Joseph Frankel

International Relations
in a Changing World

Oxford New York Toronto Melbourne

OXFORD UNIVERSITY PRESS

OPUS General Editors
Keith Thomas
Alan Ryan
Peter Medawar

Oxford University Press, Walton Street, Oxford OX2 6DP

London Glasgow New York Toronto
Delhi Bombay Calcutta Madras Karachi
Kuala Lumpur Singapore Hong Kong Tokyo
Nairobi Dar es Salaam Cape Town
Melbourne Auckland

and associated companies in
Beirut Berlin Ibadan Mexico City Nicosia

Oxford is a trade mark of Oxford University Press.

International Relations was first published in 1964
second edition 1969
International Relations in a Changing World
first published as an Oxford University Press paperback 1979
Reprinted 1981, 1983

British Library Cataloguing in Publication Data
Frankel, Joseph
International relations in a changing world
— 3rd ed. — (Opus).
1. International relations
1. Title   II. International relations
327   JX1391   79-40082
ISBN 0–19–289128–6

Printed in Great Britain by
The Guernsey Press Co. Ltd.
Guernsey, Channel Islands

Contents

Preface

Books on international relations appear in a bewildering variety and profusion: some are brief, like this one; others are long and detailed. They generally focus on one of several different elements of the international system: the system itself or the states; power, perceptions, values, conflicts and war, economics, and so on. There is little agreement among the writers and the scholars either about substance or method. The sole exception is the basic nature of the international reality which they purport to analyse and reflect: they all agree that it is complex and confusing. Nevertheless, it is difficult, at times impossible, to express all the uncertainties; however careful the author may be in his conceptualizations and interpretations, he cannot help presenting them as fairly firm—otherwise his text would become confusingly cluttered by qualifications and by alternative interpretations.

To avoid misunderstandings, I would like at the very outset to state the major goals and characteristics of my analysis. To start with, I do not aim at the presentation either of a theory of my subject, as many theoretically-minded writers do, or of its 'reality', towards which the historians strive. Mine is a merely tentative and subjective but, I hope, intelligible and common-sensical 'model', that is a way of looking at reality, which leaves open the employment of other ways deemed suitable. Second, my method is mainly analytical: I refer to a variety of historical examples, but as mere illustrating devices and not as proofs for my contentions. I do not, however, attempt to employ what some call 'scientific', especially quantitative methods; these do not appear to be suited to the analysis of many major elements of international relations and nobody has been able to apply them to the field as a whole. Third, my analysis is predominantly descriptive and not normative; it is about the world as I see it and not about one I would like to see. Only when the trends observed appear to be powerful and lasting may I border on prediction and, when functional needs appear to be overwhelming, I may come close to prescription. Finally, although I am fully aware of the need to adjust my perspectives when thinking about those governing the outlooks prevalent elsewhere, I cannot fully escape the influence of my own cultural bias, stemming from the perspective of a Western, industrialized, liberal/democratic society.

Although this volume follows the arrangement of *International Relations*, first published in this series in 1964, and reproduces, in a modified form, some of its passages, it is essentially a new book. Hence it is distinctively named rather than being published as a revised edition. In the first instance, it reflects the changes in the international system: the rise in the numbers and importance of new states, of multinational corporations and of terrorist groups; the shift of the main danger spots geographically, from Europe to the Middle East and Africa, and, functionally, from the strategic to the economic field; the growing recognition of the need for some form of global or regional regimes, overriding sovereign states. Moreover, the analysis reflects the development in my thinking about the subject, to some extent parallel to the development in the literature on theories of international relations. In my estimate these have been insufficient to affect my basic approach. Hence I have altered only the emphasis and the presentation of the individual aspects of the field, but have included a brief survey of them in the concluding chapter.

Avington, Hants.
August 1978

1 How to think about international relations

Thinking about International Relations shares to a high degree the problems of thinking about any other area of social life. The intention of the author is to avoid an exposition of the methods of social sciences which would be, by necessity, both lengthy and controversial, and instead merely to enumerate some useful categories of thinking which are currently referred to in the text.

First, by their very nature, all social phenomena exhibit both some general characteristics which they share with other phenomena, opening opportunities for classification and categorization, and some specific characteristics which are unique to them. Although this book, like all political scientific treatments, stresses the general, no full understanding of any single phenomenon can be complete without the knowledge also of its unique characteristics which are the focus of interest of the historians. Second, everything in social life is, in a direct or at least indirect way, interconnected, and all analysis has to define both the boundaries of its subject and its linkage with the context. Third, as justifiably stressed in dialectical analysis, social reality is generally characterized by the coexistence of opposed characteristics: conflict runs parallel with co-operation, strength parallel with weakness, and any analysis which excludes either is incomplete. While the statement of the opposites is analytically useful, real-life situations are, however, usually more realistically structured by regarding them as placeable within a 'spectrum' of situations between the two extremes.

Fourth, social phenomena are so complex that any simple explanation of them is, on the whole, grossly misleading. It is important to bear in mind that, however convincing the causal nexus between two phenomena may be, there are usually other significant 'causes'; in fact in many instances the uncertainty is best met by omitting the notion of causation altogether and by thinking instead about correlations. Fifth, the structuring of reality can be either static, i.e. stating it as it is at a given point in time, or dynamic, representing change. The state of international theory does not offer a firm basis for a fully-fledged dynamic model and therefore a basically static one is adopted, representing the state of affairs towards the end of the seventies, with some indication of its likely dynamism. Somewhat connected is the frequently adopted distinction between 'structure'—characteristic relationships among actors across time—and 'process'—more ephemeral forms and modes of interaction. As structure is the more basic one of the two, it is treated in much greater detail.

It is clearly impossible to incorporate all these and any additional characteristics in any single approach as the resulting model would be much too complex to be useful and, moreover, we would have great difficulties in deciding about the priorities and the relationships between the different categories. Nonetheless, it is important that we state as clearly as possible the reasons why we choose some questions as being major and seek to answer them, while others are stated as major but defy an answer and others again, though frequently regarded as major, are altogether omitted. If, as often happens, analysis were limited to what is explicable, particularly in precise quantified terms, the resulting analysis would defy common-sense conceptions of reality. This often happens, for instance, with the attempts to explain the phenomenon of 'power' in terms of concrete 'capabilities' whereas the elusive psychological elements involved are omitted, as discussed in Chapter 7.

This brings us to the issue of methodology which, as may well be expected, is highly controversial. The choice of methodology, although often argued in terms of its rational advantages over its rivals, is generally no more than a matter of individual preference dictated by personal history, temperament, and similar idiosyncratic elements. To my mind, our judgements on broad social issues are subjective and, on the whole, intuitive, but when based on sound observation and analysis and when clearly articulated, they become intelligible to others and thus inter-personal. Contrary to some modern writers, I think that only minor phenomena are amenable to 'scientific' analysis, paralleling that employed in natural sciences which is objective because its processes are not personal. It is important to stress that all that follows does not aspire to the status of scientifically established, objective 'truth'. It is no more than a statement of the subjective perceptions of reality by the author, aspiring to come as close as possible to the perceptions of the actual participants in the processes of international relations, such as diplomats, politicians, international civil servants, the military, and business men engaged in international transactions.

Writers show a fair degree of agreement about what phenomena are sufficiently important to warrant discussion but not about their relative importance. Nobody is likely to contend that geography is not a constant factor in determining events or that the accumulation of collective experience embodied in history does not determine both the national values and processes. Nevertheless, the treatment of these two constant forces varies enormously from book to book and the same is true about such generally accepted important variables as power and capabilities, perceptions, values and interests, etc. On two basic methodological issues there is a general agreement. First, one should make a distinction and be careful to separate the various levels of analysis and make clear whether one talks about the 'micro-level'-states and other units, or the 'macro-level', the international system as a whole. This is the basis of the division of this book into two parts: Chapters 2–6 and 7–11.

Second, we must come to grips with the issue of the delimitation of and the relationship between domestic politics, i.e. politics within individual states, and international politics, i.e. politics among states, however difficult it frequently is to draw a clear distinction between them. Indeed, the most important issues, whether predominantly domestic or international, are not entirely either. For example, defence expenditure hinges largely on international insecurity but also on the funds available at home; wage policy affects primarily the pockets of the individual but has important repercussions on export prices and hence on the country's foreign trade.

As in life the two domains overlap; it is therefore understandable that people trying to comprehend international affairs of which they have no direct experience or thorough knowledge, should resort to analogies from domestic politics. Here everybody is to some extent an expert: however uneducated he may be, he has some knowledge of the life and the traditions of his own country; he can reasonably guess the thoughts and reactions of his countrymen; through the mere possession of voting qualifications he participates in the political process. Unfortunately these analogies can be wrong; all the domestic expertise is of little use when applied to international affairs; in fact it can be outright misleading.

To start with, the study of the politics of other *states* presents considerable problems. We are all culture-bound, and persons quite well-versed in the politics of their own country do not necessarily understand the politics of others, based as they are on different cultures and traditions; in fact they often disregard the differences or consider them as unnatural deviations from their own national norms. Even residents in a foreign country, who are intimately acquainted with it, are often prone to misjudgements due to their different origin, as can be amply demonstrated by the frequently mistaken views of many expatriates, the 'old hands', on the countries of their sojourn. Moreover, it is easy to forget how much points of view differ according to whether one is inside or outside the country. Citizens are naturally interested mainly in the domestic affairs of their country while foreigners are equally naturally interested mainly in its foreign policy. It does not require much effort to imagine how different the resulting images are. Both the American 'capitalist' and the Soviet 'Communist' societies appear to be peace-loving to their own citizens who are impressed by domestic policies aiming at the attainment of economic and social goals; both appear aggressive to the citizens of the opposite number who think primarily of their foreign policies which are much less peaceful.

If it is hard to understand other states, it is even harder to understand *international society* as a whole. To start with, this society does not consist of individuals but of states and other group-actors. However sophisticated our approach may be, we still tend to be misled by linguistic usage and to consider states not as mental constructs, which they are, but as real entities. We *speak* about the relations between Britain and the United States as if they were relations between two persons, and therefore we tend to *think* about them in the same way, even employing the simplified graphic images of John Bull and Uncle Sam. It is just as easy to slip into the error of considering the two countries as personified in their representatives, the President and the Prime Minister, or the Secretaries of State and of Foreign Affairs. The briefest reflection will indicate the dangers of forgetting the full implications of the artificial, conventional nature of states and other group-actors and of the important differences between persons acting in their official capacities and as private individuals.

Since the language of politics has been coined within the domestic sphere, its extension to international relations easily leads to analogies which are not fully warranted. We speak of international society and of international organizations as if they were groupings of people; we discuss the international equivalents of law and morality; we discern the rights and duties of states; we analyse the organs of international institutions in terms analogous to the traditional three branches of government. Needless to say, all these analogies are defective. To a professional lawyer, international law is a very peculiar type of law; the application to the behaviour of states of moral codes developed for the individual incessantly breaks down; the ambiguities of the concept of group rights are best demonstrated in the dangerous effects of the principle of 'national self-determination', the international equivalent of the 'freedom of the individual'; the comparison of the General Assembly of the United Nations with a legislature, or of the Security Council with a government, makes little sense, and even the less far-fetched analogies between the United Nations Secretariat and a national civil service, or between the International Court of Justice and national courts, should be approached very cautiously.

These difficulties of institutional analysis are repeated in the theory and philosophy of politics. From the earliest traditions of ancient Greece, thinkers have been concerned mainly with state governments, with the relations between the individual and authority. Theories and philosophies have been devised for a society of men which can be advanced either through the improvement of its members, or of the social order, or of both, and to which the concept of 'justice' can be meaningfully applied. They have only limited application to a society of states where each member incessantly confronts other intractable members, and hence is concerned primarily with its survival and is subject to the dictates of necessity. Many continental thinkers, from Machiavelli onwards, noted this fundamental difference but, on the background of their long tradition of national security and of the 'moral opportunity' arising from it, many British and American thinkers neglected international relations. Only the growing interdependence since the Second World War has made the linkage between domestic and international politics obvious.

Somewhat independently of the mainstream of political thought, diplomats and international lawyers have developed a common language, a set of common traditions with a specifically international content, such concepts as 'balance of power', which belong fully to the international sphere. Unfortunately, although these traditions are still cherished by some Western diplomats and lawyers, their application is rather limited. International society as we know it today has come into being only in the post-war years: over half of its members, the Afro-Asian states, are newcomers to the international stage, while the two Superpowers, the United States and the Soviet Union, are relative newcomers to their exalted status. Clearly categories and norms developed within the predominantly European context of the international society of the nineteenth century could scarcely be of general application today.

In our century, the growing popular interest in the relations among states has led to the development of a new specialized branch of knowledge, usually described by the name earlier coined by Jeremy Bentham as 'International Relations'. This new discipline is more than a combination of the studies of the foreign affairs of the various countries and of international history—it includes also the study of international society as a whole and of its institutions and processes. It is increasingly concerned not only with the states and their interactions but also with the web of transnational politics. In a way, the term 'World Politics', employed by some writers, describes its contents more truthfully than the traditional name 'International Relations'.

No general theory of international relations commands widespread acceptance and the subsequent discussion is not based on any individual theory. However, in order to generalize about the relations of over one hundred and fifty states, all different in size, power, and other attributes, and all acting against the backgrounds of their individual national traditions, it is necessary to have at least some working hypothesis or model. The difficulty lies in accommodating the conflicting patterns of international politics: it is impossible to deal with the subject without emphasizing either the role of states or of the transnational processes or of the international system; either conflict or co-operation;[1] either the clear but disappearing patterns of the past or the vague and merely hypothetical trends for the future.

The pattern of the past is still prominent. Mankind is loosely organized into an international society of sovereign states which have the near monopoly of power and to a large extent rely on power in their mutual relations. These states are represented by individuals holding certain official positions who determine state policies under the complex, often conflicting influences and pressures from their domestic and international environments. Inevitably this international society is subject to repeated crises and to the recurrent danger of a major war, although the slowly growing co-operation among states and, even more so, the growing volume of transnational activities, give some hope for an advance towards a greater degree of international order.

This model is neither particularly original nor profound, but it is useful and flexible. It not only provides a realistic approach to the study of the 'behaviour of states' through that of the behaviour of their representatives, but it also accommodates both the facts of the world of sovereign states governed mainly by power politics and the many phenomena of the contemporary world which cannot be fitted into this mould. It allows full scope for the co-operative trends which encourage hope for the order of tomorrow. Any reasonable treatment must be able to do that in order to do justice to our confused period of transition.

[1] J. Frankel, *International Politics: Conflict and Harmony*, Penguin, 1969.

2 States I

The structure of international society

Writers on international relations agree that the structure of international society is becoming increasingly complex, but they violently disagree about the most helpful way of looking at it. The traditional way was to concentrate upon the states as the historically prominent units, and to ignore other agents (or, as they are now often called, actors) lacking, as they do, the basic characteristics of states—their sovereignty and their territoriality, on which later. The influence of the post-war evolution of behavioural sciences has led to a greater or lesser acceptance of a behavioural analysis of the international system as consisting of numerous, more or less autonomous interacting actors. In order to make up for the omissions of the traditionalists, many innovators have been excessively concentrating upon the crisis of the traditional states and/or upon the newly arisen non-state actors.

In order to restore the balance, it seems advisable to combine the two modes of analysis. We should think of the international system as one combining several kinds of actors of varying degrees of autonomy in their international behaviour, with the states among them retaining a leading but by no means exclusive or uniform role. The difficulties of analysing such a multi-actor system are, however, immense, and, in practice, authors tend to concentrate either upon state or upon non-state actors. Concentration upon either class inevitably precludes a balanced analysis of the international system as a whole and therefore an attempt will be made here to avoid such restriction and to do justice to both types. The non-state actors are, however, given much less prominence than the states, for two connected reasons: first, they are behaviourally less significant and, second, their analysis has not been developed nearly as adequately as that of states. There is, however, included some factual information about them because it may not be otherwise readily accessible.

To start with, it seems to be useful to attempt a common framework for looking at all the actors, both states and non-states, from the angle of their positions in the international system. In order to achieve this it is necessary to bear in mind at least the following four basic dimensions, developed in the analysis of states but equally applicable to other actors:

1. *Orientation towards participation* in the international system. There is a wide spectrum of possible policies between the extremes of full participation in the web of world politics, characterizing the United States, and the relative isolationism of contemporary Burma or Nepal; a similar spectrum could be developed for multinational corporations (M.N.C.s) or terrorist movements.

2. *Scope*, which can be understood as a geographical dimension, with actors dividing into those with mainly global, regional, subregional, and more local scope, and functional, according to the fields of international interaction in which they participate. While non-state actors have, as a rule, a limited functional scope, states have a potentially fully comprehensive multi-functional scope. Individual states do not, however, necessarily exercise it: they sometimes withdraw from the security interactions by deliberate policies of neutrality or isolationism or, as Japan and China, Burma and Cambodia have all in turn demonstrated, they can do likewise in the field of international trade.

3. *Power*, which must be clearly defined both in functional and in relative terms specifying what the power purports to achieve and in relations with whom. This merges into the somewhat overlapping category of *influence*—the ability to achieve the desired ends. The best way to clarify the confused relationship between these two concepts is to regard power as a potential of influence.

4. *Domestic structure* relevant for international interaction. One element is readily discernible—the decision-making institutions. There are, however, other, less clear-cut but very important aspects: stability and capacity for adaptation to change, taking into account the nature of challenges at home and abroad; legitimacy—manifesting itself as loyalty of citizens at home and of friends and allies abroad, etc.

The development of the state-system

Modern states and modern international society are only a very recent phenomenon. The three or four centuries of their history are only a small fraction of the more than seven thousand years of the recorded history of man and a proportionately smaller fraction of his very much longer biological history. Yet international relations were foreshadowed a long time ago.

In its broadest historical perspective, the present state-system is best explained by Aristotle's celebrated observation that man is by nature a political animal. At all stages of development, people have needs and wants which they cannot realize alone, and hence they form social groups. Such groups differ greatly in their nature and scope, according to circumstances, but they invariably strike a host of organizational problems pertaining to the structure of the group, and also to its relationships with other groups, the equivalent of modern international relations. One fundamental problem here is that of delimitation, of finding the size best suited for the purposes of the group. Plato and Aristotle discuss it in their analyses of the Greek city-states; modern sociologists are concerned with it whether they develop theories of social communication or of areas of loyalty or of relations between the 'ingroup' and the 'outgroup'. Also, economists are concerned with economics of size and, recently, with the question of whether 'small is beautiful'.

In fact something approaching international relations can be read into the social behaviour of animals which is now being re-interpreted by zoologists. Groupings of animals are determined by considerations of biological survival; they must secure food and breeding-ground and hence are capable of fierce intra-species conflicts which generally revolve around the exclusive use of territory for breeding and for feeding and the exclusion of trespassers likely to compete for the use of its facilities.

Most analyses of human organization start with an assumption about the original state of nature, describing it either as a state of innocence, a Golden Age, or as a Hobbesian war of all against all. For the purposes of this discussion it is unnecessary to decide in favour of either view. Whether man was originally motivated by sentiments of sympathy or of hostility, or by a mixture of both, he soon discovered that co-operation within a group provided benefits, and also that the contacts of his own group with other groups affected his interests, either positively or negatively, or, confusingly, both. We can only speculate about the development of relations among primitive groups. Possibly, while they were few, men simply avoided contacts, but it is plausible to assume that, with growing numbers and with increasing sophistication, such contacts soon grew. If an analogy with the animal world suggests that the first contacts may have been hostile, already in pre-history some non-violent forms of inter-group relations were established and institutionalized (e.g. heralds were endowed with immunity) and mutually advantageous trade exchanges took place. Once such relations had reached a certain frequency and intensity, they became an important incentive to establish an efficient central government within the group to control them.

They required also some minimum conditions for intercourse between groups—some degree of linguistic understanding and probably also of religious community, sufficient at least to trust the oaths sworn by the other side. Thus the perennial dilemma of international relations faced man already in pre-history. When a group is no longer self-sufficient, when some of its vital needs can be satisfied only from the outside, is it preferable to ensure their satisfaction through the subjugation of the other groups involved or through some form of inter-group co-operation and exchange? The choice between war and peaceful coexistence is painful, since both carry their risks. Military conquest is the simpler method and, indeed, it seems to have been the rule throughout history, although we must allow for the likely tendency of the scanty early records to refer to the spectacular military feats of rulers rather than to the unspectacular flow of peaceful intercourse such as international trade.

It is possible to interpret the political history of mankind as an age-long series of attempts to determine the size of supreme social groupings suitable for the circumstances of the time and the place. While unifying forces led to empires based upon conquest or to confederations based upon consent, separatist forces invariably reasserted themselves, causing the disintegration of the larger units. Undoubtedly in many vital respects the whole globe has now become one area of activity, but it does not necessarily follow that the forces of unity will inevitably score a permanent victory. Few people would accept today Sir Halford Mackinder's thesis of geo-graphical compulsion that 'the grouping of lands and seas, and of fertility and natural pathways, is such as to lend itself to the growth of empires, and in the end of a single World Empire'.[1] The nuclear menace, modern communications, economic interdependence *could* lead to the integration of the world either by conquest or by growing co-operation, but there is nothing inevitable about the process nor any assurance that, even if it succeeds, unity would remain permanent.

The first large-scale political organizations, states, and state-systems of which we possess records, developed about 5000 B.C. in the Tigris-Euphrates and Nile valleys and somewhat later in the valleys of the great rivers of China. Their location was not due to accident but to a social need common to all these areas. They all required strong centralized organizations capable of constructing and maintaining irrigation systems which were indispensable for food production. Professor Karl Wittfogel has developed a plausi-ble theory about the resulting despotic character of these societies which he called 'hydraulic'.[2]

Growing numbers and sophistication were incessantly increas-ing the range of human needs and were leading, although jerkily, to larger human groupings. First in the valleys of the great rivers and then in larger areas, states became enmeshed in networks of inter-state relations alternating between the two patterns of sepa-rate warring and co-operating units, and of great empires imposed upon them. These political systems, usually called civilizations, were fluctuating in their boundaries, but were geographically fairly segregated from one another; each developed a degree of cultural and political coherence. On the whole, contacts among them were sporadic although some were of great cultural impor-tance. The intrepid scholars, missionaries, and travellers who crossed the formidable Gobi desert in the early centuries of our era brought Buddhism from India to China; oriental influences intro-duced by Alexander the Great altered the character of Greek civilization; the 'barbarians' who harried the Chinese and the

---

[1] Sir Halford Mackinder, *Democratic Ideals and Reality*, London, 1909.
[2] K. Wittfogel, *Oriental Despotism: a Comparative Study of Totalitarian Power*, Yale University Press, 1957.

Roman Empires were not only enemies of these civilizations but also creative elements which became assimilated to the former and rebuilt the latter in the form of the medieval Christian Commonwealth; in our century, anthropological studies of primitive people have opened our eyes to many problems of our own.

In the eastern Mediterranean, civilizations interacted more intensely and occasionally came into dramatic conflict. From the unfortunate position of their small buffer-state between the Assyrians and the Egyptians, the Hebrew prophets recorded the clash between the two empires which began in the fourteenth century B.C.; in the fifth century B.C. the Persians invaded Greece, and in the following century Alexander invaded the Orient; the Middle Ages witnessed a prolonged conflict between the Christians and the Moslems. Until the second half of the fifteenth century A.D., however, Europe and the Middle East remained almost wholly separated from the large organized civilizations in China and in India as well as from the other, less organized continents.

Our image of the international society of today as having arisen mainly from the background of Western history is partly culture-bound in its origins, but is, nevertheless, of general validity. It is a historical fact that, owing to its superior technology and political organization, from the fifteenth century onwards European civilization gradually extended its rule all over the globe. Today, when other civilizations and continents have successfully asserted themselves against Europe, their own histories and traditions have assumed an obvious importance, but only as additions and corrections to the existing system. Throughout the world, science and technology, political institutions, culture-bearing languages, the very idea of a society of sovereign interacting states—all have their origins in Europe.

Being conducted within an international society or system, international relations imply a multitude of units separate in some respects but constituting a whole in others—the result of an interplay between unitary and particularist forces. This interplay can be employed as the focus for the study of the rich and varied Western heritage; the subsequent few paragraphs will indicate a way in which this can be done.

The Greeks, who devised the vocabulary of domestic politics, were less inventive for international relations, although they clearly distinguished some features which are characteristic of the modern state-system, such as bipolarity and balance of power among sovereign states. While jealously preserving the independence of their city-states, they recognized a degree of unity in Greece as a whole and developed such common institutions as the Amphictyonic Council and the Olympic Games; they distinguished between conflicts within their own system (*stasis*) and wars from outsiders (*polemos*). The Romans epitomized the idea of unity in the ingenious institutions of their Empire which tolerated cultural divergencies as long as these were not politically dangerous. The medieval Christian Commonwealth successfully, although not very effectively, preserved the *idea* of unity through the institutions of the Church, the Empire, and the Universities, while a chaotic multitude of local political units gradually combined into several hierarchically arranged loose feudal systems. The medieval order eventually crumbled under the impact of the Renaissance and the Reformation.

With the disappearance of religious unity, particularist forces reasserted themselves. For a while both the Catholic and the Reformed Churches clung to the idea of medieval unity based on a common faith and endeavoured to impose their respective creeds on the whole of Europe. The local princes who rose to political importance through the accumulation and the ruthless use of power became immersed in religious wars, both fighting for their creeds abroad and trying to ensure their complete sway at home. As Machiavelli rightly observed, modern states were based on power; however, their religious origin must not be neglected. Religious forces did not disappear from politics completely but, in the form of national churches, generally adapted themselves to the new units.

The resulting system of sovereign territorial states, which was formally established by the Peace Treaty of Westphalia in 1648, was at first limited to Europe. Gradually, however, European states extended their rule over other continents which they considered fair game for their expansion. In one sense, by including overseas territories within their empires, they spread the diversity of the European state-system over the whole globe. In another sense, they united the world physically, by opening communications, and culturally, by spreading European culture. Early in the twentieth century the system became threatened by several challenges. The empire-building process which was essential for the functioning of the European community came to an end when there were no more continents to annex and people to subjugate; Great Powers—the United States and Japan—arose outside Europe; under the impact of nationalism, non-European peoples began to act more independently. Although still predominantly European, the inter-war international organization, the League of Nations, was, at least in concept, universal. The final blow to unity was caused by the gradual dissociation of the system from its Christian origins and by the split between the three offspring of Western tradition—liberal democracy, communism, and fascism.

During its course, the Second World War was generally thought to be the defence of the system against its most dangerous adversary and, for some time afterwards, the forces for unity appeared to be on the march, admittedly not in favour of world-wide but rather of bloc integration. It seemed likely that the smaller states would become gradually absorbed into the orbits of the United States and the Soviet Union, the two Superpowers which had arisen in the wake of the war. The envisaged bipolar world has not, however, materialized. The nuclear stalemate seems to neutralize the two Superpowers and to enable other states to assert themselves, whether they are uncommitted and neutral or dependent. Instead of a bipolarity based upon blocs integrated around the two Superpowers, a world-wide polycentric system has been gradually shaping, a system subdivided into Western, Communist, and third world sub-systems within which the separate state-units can act fairly independently. While the forces of unity have not prevailed within the blocs, they are operating, although in a very attenuated form, in the United Nations, which is world-wide. Simultaneously transnational forces began to assert themselves and important non-state actors began to rise.

In the last few decades, particularly since 1945, international society has undergone important changes, but its basic structure has remained the same since 1648, especially in its theoretical foundations; it is a society of sovereign territorial states. Consequently it is necessary to start with the analysis of the 'classical' international society and its member-states and to postpone the discussion of the evolution in this century. This approach emphasizes diversity, which is embodied in these states and has been prominent for the last three centuries. The forces of unity, however, have never fully disappeared and will be discussed in Chapters 8–11.

A word may be added about the implications of the highly dynamic nature of international society. Social forces operating within it change all the time in their nature but not in the mode of their operation. The metaphor of the swing of the pendulum is here quite illuminating, provided we accept that the swing changes from beat to beat, both in its extent and in its speed. If we apply this metaphor to the interaction between the forces of unity and of particularism, the unity achieved under the Roman Empire meant that the pendulum reached one extreme position and then slowly, but in the last stages, with catastrophic speed, swung to the particularism of the Dark Ages. The Holy Roman Empire consti-tuted merely a feeble swing towards unity, and was again followed by the extreme particularism established at Westphalia. There is little doubt that the forces of unity have been building up since then, but the extent of the swing and its present momentum are difficult to ascertain.

Elements of statehood

At the outset the fact must be stressed that states, being the most extensive and comprehensive units of human organization, are extremely complex. Hence they show quite different features when considered in their different capacities, either as political organiza-tions of governmental authority in their relations with the citizens, or as economic, social, or cultural structures. By necessity the discussion of states here focuses around the role they play in inter-national society; consequently many of their otherwise important characteristics can be barely touched upon or even mentioned and only the elements of the state structure directly relevant for rela-tions with other states are discussed. A convenient starting point may be found in the formal legal approach. According to the British authority on international law, L. Oppenheim, a state 'is in existence when a people is settled in a country under its own sovereign government'.[1] This definition includes four distinct elements: a people, a territory, a government, and the attribute of sovereignty.

The people

Since states are a form of social organization, this is obviously an essential element. The people are an aggregate of both sexes living in a community which need not be homogeneous. The size of the group is not fixed: there are close to a thousand million people in Communist China while the people of the smallest states are counted in thousands. However, most jurists agree that there is some lower limit to the size of a people and they have doubts about the statehood of such tiny groups as Liechtenstein or Andorra, and deny the existence of conditions for a separate statehood of the smallest surviving colonial territories. Of course all these small groups are generally poorly equipped also in other essential elements of statehood.

The territory

Perhaps the most important characteristic of the modern state, distinguishing it from the medieval order, is its territoriality. This feature, sometimes described as impermeability or impenetrability, can be considered as the basic ingredient of the modern state: its strategic aspects are usually included in the analysis of state power, the political aspects are described as independence, and the legal ones as sovereignty.

The origin of the territorial state lies in the 'gunpowder revolution' which destroyed the security of the medieval castles and cities and resulted in a shift of the 'hard shell' of impenetrability from walls and moats to the broader confines of state-boundaries. When neither local defences nor the Popes and Emperors could provide security, the Princes, the rulers of larger territories, became its best guarantors and their states became the basic units. We can consider the rise of the modern territorial state as a triumph of particularism over medieval unity, or as a partial victory of unity over the anarchy and disorder of the Middle Ages. On either interpreta-

[1] L. Oppenheim, *International Law*, Vol. I, Seventh edition. 1952.

tion, the modern territorial state is based on the twin elements of internal pacification and of external defensibility.

Territories of states vary in size as much as do their populations. The largest state in existence, the Soviet Union, covers an area of approximately 8.5 million square miles but some states measure only a few thousand or even a few hundred square miles.

The government

The government consists of one or more persons who represent the people and rule according to the law of the land. Since all states conduct their foreign affairs through their governments, an anarchist community, even if it could exist on a sufficiently large scale, would not qualify as a state. After the October Revolution in 1917, the Bolshevik rulers tried to do away with their foreign ministry and to replace inter-governmental relations with direct relations with other peoples, but they soon gave up their futile attempt and their Utopian 'withering away' of the state has not materialized. Governments play a crucial part in the making of foreign policy on behalf of their states, and hence their structures and mode of operation are discussed in some detail in Chapter 4.

Theoretically, sovereign governments are in full control both of the domestic and of the foreign affairs of their countries, but here, as on some other issues, a sharp distinction must be drawn between the two. As long as a government is recognized as such by other governments, it remains the legal reresentative of its country, even if its control over it is severely challenged or completely lost. Thus, for a long period, the Nationalist Government of China remained recognized by the United States and by several other states as the Government of the whole of China despite the fact that, since 1949, its rule was limited to Taiwan and a few small islands; during the Second World War, the governments-in-exile in London retained the recognition of Britain and the United States although they were temporarily divorced from the other elements of statehood. The obverse is likewise true—that groups organized as governments may be in actual control of a territory and yet remain unrecognized. Discrepancy between recognition and actual control leads to difficulties in international intercourse but may persist for a number of years. For instance, after 1945 the United States did not recognize the Government of Communist

China or the incorporation, in 1940, into the Soviet Union of the three small Baltic states, Lithuania, Latvia, and Estonia; despite its full qualification as an independent state, Southern Rhodesia never enjoyed recognition throughout its existence after the Unilateral Declaration of Independence in 1965 because its government was regarded as illegitimate.

Sovereignty

There are many definitions of sovereignty and much confusion is caused by the emotional content of the word, but there is general agreement that the sovereignty of states is important. On the one hand, sovereignty has been described as 'the supreme political characteristic' or 'the central legal formula' of international society; on the other, its allegedly obsolete nature has been blamed for the major ills of contemporary international life.

In fact sovereignty expresses an important political reality, but is not absolute and does not necessarily impede the integration of states into larger units. Sovereignty means supreme authority which recognizes no superior and beyond which there is no legal appeal. This basic meaning has remained unchanged throughout modern times and Jean Bodin's definition made in 1576 that sovereignty is 'the supreme power over citizens and subjects unrestrained by law' has remained valid even though Bodin's sovereign absolutist ruler has now been replaced by the nation.

Again we must draw a distinction between the domestic and the international spheres because 'sovereignty' gives rise to different problems in each. The classical problems of internal sovereignty such as the source and justification of the supreme power, its relation with the citizens, its location, and the question of whether it can be divided, need not detain us long. In international relations, sovereignty is accepted as a fact and governments are considered as representatives of their states, wherever political scientists and jurists may locate the ultimate sovereign power. External sovereignty can be divided, as shown by the historical cases of such 'semi-sovereignties' as protectorates, or the Free City of Danzig in the inter-war period, or the Free Territory of Trieste between 1945 and 1954, or by the still existing case of Monaco. In substance, however, in all these instances the semi-sovereign state has no supreme authority to conduct its foreign affairs, and hence is not really sovereign at all.

External sovereignty implies a basic contradiction of any notion of international order. An international society of fully sovereign states is just as unthinkable as a domestic anarchist society of fully sovereign individuals. Since law is the formal expression of social order, this contradiction shows most clearly in the relations between the institutions of the sovereign state and of international law.

International law establishes norms of social behaviour in the same way as does law within a state—or, as the lawyers call it, municipal law—but it is a much weaker kind of law precisely because its subjects, the states, are sovereign. International law is based on two apparently contradictory assumptions: first, that the states, being sovereign, are basically not subject to any legal restraint; second, that international law does impose such restraints. Obviously neither assumption is fully tenable: neither can the state's external authority be quite unlimited, otherwise there would be no law at all, nor can we expect the legal order to be centralized and strong. The principle of 'consent' enables us to reconcile this basic contradiction, at least in theory: in the exercise of their sovereignty, states can and do bind themselves to observe certain rules and contract certain obligations. Thus the rules of international law which they have accepted, explicitly or implicitly, do not derive from a superior authority above states, which would contradict their sovereign character, but are made by the states themselves. Consequently, international law is a law among states and not above them. Specifically, the states often agree to limit their sovereignty through the conclusion of innumerable international agreements and through their membership of international institutions.

Social coherence, nationalism, and legitimacy

Some lawyers argue that a state exists as soon as the four formal elements can be found in it, and that recognition by other states merely recognizes this social fact. Others argue that such recognition is constitutive, that it is only through receiving such recognition that the state assumes its identity as a member of international society. On the former theory, the formal elements are deemed sufficient; on the latter, recognition is required in addition, and is in fact the most important element since it can be granted even if the formal elements are defective or refused when they exist. A sociological investigation of the issue of the state's 'legitimacy' offers a convenient tool for analysing both the domestic and the international aspects of recognition.

To start with the domestic angle, we must try to explain how the formal elements of statehood are fused, what endows the government with legitimacy in the eyes of its people and ensures its domestic sovereignty, what holds society together. The government's primary task is to organize the political life of the country and hence it concentrates political power. Some of the newly established states have been recognized as such on the basis of this political organization alone, although the social, economic, and cultural ties characterizing older states simply do not exist in them. It is, however, a historical fact that all states within the classical political system have either started with or achieved such ties and that modern governments wield a considerable amount not only of political, but also of economic and social power. Deficiencies in these non-political bonds must be taken into account when assessing the position and the prospects of the new states.

Even political power, which is the very basis of the recognition of the government by other states, cannot be taken for granted. The concentration of political power in the hands of the government is the rule, but not a rule without exceptions: it may be challenged by separatist forces, insurgents may arise and take over part of the state's territory, aggressors may occupy it, regional and minority allegiances may prevail against loyalty to the state. Especially with new states, we must check in every single case the extent of the actual political powers of the government; there are many examples of such powers being highly deficient.

Ever since the French Revolution nationalism has been the main spiritual and emotional force cementing all the elements of statehood in nation-states, and these have become the classical type of unit. Wherever the nation-state was a reality, nationalism buttressed and reinforced the state; where it remained an aspiration, nationalism endangered the existing multinational units. Hence the relations between the state and the nation require careful consideration. The close historical links between the two concepts date back only just over a century and a half and we would not be justified in considering them as perennial. Unfortunately confusion arises from linguistic usage. As the noun 'state' in English is rigid and precludes the formation of derivatives, we use substitutes formed from the more flexible word 'nation'. Thus 'international law' and 'international relations' are the accepted terms for the law and relations among states; 'nationalization' describes the acquisition of enterprise by the state. Although international law is the term used in other languages, too, generally these languages are less rigid and they permit more accurate terminology such as *étatisation* or *Verstaatlichung* for nationalization.

Not only are states and nations not identical but the links between them vary greatly in time and place. Sometimes states precede nations, as in Western Europe, sometimes nations precede states, as in Central and Eastern Europe. At present, states of vastly different nature are multinational, for instance the Soviet Union, Switzerland, and Malaysia; other states have large national minorities; some nations are divided into separate states, for instance the Germans, the Koreans, and, for a while, also the Vietnamese. Relations between the state and the nation cannot be equated with those between the state and society because in no state is this society limited to the members of one nation alone, nor is any nation limited to society within a single state.

If by a community we understand a social group within which men live all their lives, as distinct from associations within which they satisfy only some of their needs, a nation is a community. It differs from other communities first of all in size: the smaller communities, the family and the village, are small face-to-face groups, whereas a nation encompasses millions or at least many thousands. Second, the nation commands the supreme loyalty of its members; third, it has become closely connected with the institution of the state.

A nation can be defined either through the objective characteristics common to its individual members or through the subjective sentiments of those members, or through a combination of both. The 1939 Report on Nationalism produced by the Royal Institute of International Affairs found the following features in most, though not in all, nations:

1. The idea of a common government, whether as a reality in the present or the past, or as an aspiration for the future.

2. A certain size and closeness of contact between all the individual members. To take the example of contemporary Africa, tribes, however conscious of their distinctness, would not qualify for nationhood because they are too small, while Pan-African sentiments and contacts are too loose to constitute an all-African nation.

3. A more or less defined territory—here the Jews before the establishment of Israel are the major exception.

4. Certain characteristics distinguishing the nations from other nations and non-national groups. Language ranks high, although there exist some multi-linguistic nations like the Belgians or the Swiss, while some languages are shared by more than one nation, like English, French, German, or Serbo-Croat. Race, religion, and national character are among the most prominent of these common characteristics.

5. Certain interests common to all individual members. Especially through the instrumentality of the state, the nation has become the purveyor of many social needs; hence belonging to a nation means sharing many specific interests as well as the fundamental interest in the perpetuation of the nation.

6. A certain degree of common feeling or will, associated with a picture of the nation in the minds of the individual members.

According to subjective definitions, nationalism is a state of mind. In his *Representative Government* (1861), John Stuart Mill stressed common sympathies among members of a nation which 'make them co-operate with each other more willingly than with other people, desire to be under the same government, and desire that it should be government by themselves or portion of themselves, exclusively'. In 1882 in an oft-quoted passage, Renan spoke of the nation as a 'soul, a spiritual principle', whose existence is a 'daily plebiscite'.

Nations do not emerge as clear-cut entities from these definitions nor are they clear-cut entities in life. Thus in the inter-war period many German-speaking Austrians considered themselves as members of the German nation whereas few do so now; the Syrians and Egyptians think of themselves as separate nations while at the same time many of them regard themselves also as members of the Arab 'nation' which was, between 1958 and 1961, embodied in the ephemeral United Arab Republic; to choose an example closer to home, most Scots are conscious of their membership both of the Scottish and of the wider British nation, with various gradations of priority.

It would, of course, be possible to focus discussion on nationalism as the major spiritual force activating mankind, to analyse its role in filling the place previously occupied by religion or to speculate on the possibilities of its replacement by ideologies. It is, however, easier to understand nationalism if it is discussed as one of the features of the relations among states. Instead of trying to analyse the vague 'excesses' of nationalism we can more concretely explore the place of nationalism within the state-system.

The first point to be borne in mind is the historical fact that nationalism was generated on the Atlantic seaboard of Western Europe, in France, England, Scotland, and Spain, and that it spread only slowly to the remainder of Europe and the Western Hemisphere, and only recently to the other continents. In the same way as socialism or trade unionism or any other idea or institution, nationalism has been changing during the course of history and means something different in different circumstances. With its traditions stretching back for more than three centuries and within the homogeneous society of contemporary Britain, nationalism obviously cannot mean the same as it does in the Congo, where it appeared only a short time ago in a society torn by regional and tribal allegiances. Much of the confusion about the meaning of nationalism stems from unwarranted generalizations.

Second, following the indecisive conclusion of the wars of religion, nationalism became the most important element in state-making. In Western Europe it legitimized and reinforced political structures which had previously come into existence; elsewhere it served as a powerful force to destroy existing structures and to establish new states roughly corresponding with nations. The emotional impact of nationalism remains unimpaired. It is possible to discover some signs of its weakening in western Europe, but the new Asian and African states are strongly nationalistic.

The rivals of nationalism have not been successful. The two World Wars in which workers rallied on the side of their own nations proved how wrong Marx had been in his expectation that the proletarians of all countries would unite, that class loyalty would prevail over national loyalty; on the contrary, nationalism has now been joined to socialism and has absorbed it. Likewise ideology merely reinforced nationalism in Fascist Italy and in Nazi Germany.

There remains the challenge of Communism. Indeed, today's ideological divisions cut across the bodies politic of such nations as the Germans, or the Koreans, and the ideologically determined 'iron curtain' is politically much more important than the boundaries between nation-states. However, these divisions are based not only upon ideology but, perhaps even more, on power relations between the Soviet Union and the United States, relations to which an analysis of the old-fashioned imperialism can be applied. Moreover, far from disappearing, nationalism reasserts itself and endangers the ideologically defined frontiers. By the end of the century our period may appear to prove not the triumph of ideology over nationalism but rather the reverse, that political patterns cutting across nations are inherently unstable, however strong the supporting ideological force may be.

Even within the ideologically dominated Soviet bloc, nationalism has raised its head in several countries, first of all in Yugoslavia, then in 1956 in Hungary and Poland, and lastly, in 1967 and 1968 in Rumania and Czechoslovakia; Chinese nationalism has prevented China's integration in the bloc and has led to a serious Sino-Soviet rift. In the Soviet Union itself, instead of merely tolerating nationalism, since the beginning of the last war, Communism has allied itself with Russian nationalism and has been trying, not entirely successfully, to submerge the other nationalisms in the Union in an all-embracing Soviet nationalism. Still, owing to its multinational character and to the high proportion—over one-half—of the non-Russian nationalities, the Soviet Union is a unique case in which ideology rather than nationalism can be considered as the main social force cementing the state.

It is, however, likewise possible to take the opposite view and to claim that the rise of the numerous Third World states has destroyed the traditional conception of the nation-state. None of these new states are nationally coherent in the Western European tradition and they are all riven by tribal, ethnic, religious, and regional differences; their boundaries do not correspond with any meaningful national boundaries and, on the whole, their strenuous efforts at 'nation-building', which their governments have been justly regarding as their primary post-independence task, have not been successful. For analytical purposes, it is possible to distinguish between four categories of motivational orientations towards the nation-state: ideological on the one hand, and functional, normative, and symbolic on the other. It is the rather uncertain prevalence of one or other of these orientations which will ultimately determine the future of the individual nation-state.

If the issue of the internal legitimacy of states to their citizens is rather unclear, the issue of their external legitimacy is, if anything, even more confused. International law has never been a decisive arbiter of recognition—the United States practice has always been openly political, granting or refusing recognition of states and governments according to the decisions of the President, whereas the British tended to recognize facts and to grant recognition following the actual exercise of authority over territory. Naturally the practical results greatly differed, e.g. in 1947 the United States immediately recognized the newly established state of Israel whereas Britain was much slower; by contrast, the British recognized the Central People's Government in China a short time after its final consolidation, whereas the Americans continued to recognize the Government of the Republic of China.

Since 1945, no longer British and United States practice but the ideological blocs and the General Assembly (G.A.) of the United Nations (U.N.) became the purveyors of legitimacy. The separate parts of the nation-states, split by the ideological divisions after 1945, commanded recognition according to the ideology of the other states: Western Germany, Southern Korea, and South Vietnam (as long as it remained in existence) were recognized by the Western bloc while their communist counterparts were recognized by the Communist bloc. The Third World established fairly clear rules about the legitimacy of the successor-states after decolonization: the states were recognized within their existing colonial boundaries and breakaway units were recognized only exceptionally, but in most cases were refused recognition, especially if support from the ex-colonial ruler or a racial minority rule were involved. Thus Ruanda and Burundi were allowed to separate into two states but not Eastern Indonesia or the Katanga (later named

Shaba) province of the Congo.

The case of Southern Rhodesia is the most prominent of the central importance of legitimacy. After its unilateral declaration of independence (U.D.I.) in 1965, the Government of Southern Rhodesia was universally denied legitimacy not only for its illegal breakaway origins but increasingly also as an oppressive racialist minority government. The legitimacy of the regime led to the declaration of mandatory sanctions against it by the U.N. and to widespread support for the independence fighters challenging it, leading to its gradual decline. This was by no means an isolated case. The international system was gradually moving towards a situation in which regimes generally regarded as reprehensible would be denied legitimacy not only at their inception but could have recognition withdrawn from them: in the late seventies, under Chinese pressure, recognition had been generally withdrawn from the Republic of China on Taiwan; South Africa came under an increasing threat of international sanctions for its racialist policy of apartheid; the Arabs, powerful as oil-exporters, were pressing hard against Israel. A new category sometimes called 'pariah states', had come into being, of states whose recognition had been withdrawn or was threatened. Although this did not preclude their continuation as states—Taiwan, for example, remained stable and prosperous—it greatly jeopardized their future.

3 States II

Classification of states

In the second half of the nineteenth century it was possible for a politician concerned with foreign policy, a diplomat, or a scholar to become acquainted in sufficient detail with the foreign policies of all the states that mattered—the five great European Powers—and to acquire sufficient knowledge of any specific trouble or danger spots arising in the world. In the inter-war world this became much more difficult as the number of states greatly grew and international politics became more global, and the difficulty has become further accentuated since 1945, when the membership of the United Nations has become three-fold that of the maximum League of Nations membership of fifty, and issues of international politics have grown in number and complexity. This is the basic justification for an analytical approach to international relations, as the detailed encyclopedic knowledge open to a nineteenth-century practitioner or scholar is no longer feasible. It is possible, and intellectually attractive, to generalize about the behaviour of all states and, indeed, some quite meaningful generalizations can be made about it, summing up all the behavioural characteristics arising from their position as states. Clearly, however, the behaviour of individual states is not only similar to that of other states but also different in many important respects. If we wish to avoid the necessity of studying in each particular case all its details and the danger that we may do so in a manner which would make comparisons with other states difficult, it is important to establish not only a clear and articulate general framework of analysis which will allow us a certain degree of generalization about all states, but also to distinguish in addition sub-classes of states which show similarities going beyond the characteristics common to all states, and thus reduce the area requiring detailed specific study for each individual case.

The simplest and justifiably popular method of classification is by geographical regions, which is the basis of area-expertise. Clearly not only a range of common problems but also of behavioural similarities peculiar to the states in the region exist in the E.E.C. area, Eastern Europe, Latin America and, within it, Central America, the Middle East, or Africa and, although to a lesser extent, also in the Far East or South-east Asia. The regional similarities can be found in different forms: some may take an institutional one, e.g. with the members of the E.E.C. channelling certain foreign policy issues through the machinery of E.E.C. consultation; some are the outcome of sharing a common foreign policy problem of overriding importance, like the relations with the adjoining Superpower; some may be largely attributed to greater intensity of interaction and to the evolution of historically established customs, as the Latin American styles of diplomacy and doctrines of international law. A similar process is probably taking place within the context of Africa and the O.A.U.

Area-similarities apply, however, primarily to area-politics and, in application to global politics, other sources of similarity are generally sought. The traditional divison used to be into the 'Great Powers' and other states, occasionally subdivided into Small and Middle Powers. Post-war literature has been increasingly less concerned with the issues of this simple classification which used to take an inordinate amount of space and energy without ever resolving the crucial issue of the yardsticks for delimitation. The basic idea of classifying states by power and status has, however, survived, and new, more sophisticated attempts were made in the post-war period, adding, however, complexity rather than precision to the old-fashioned classification. Well-known is the one which has been proposed by James N. Rosenau in his 'pretheory' of foreign policy, first publicly discussed in 1964. It is based on the plausible assumption that some domestic attributes of states can be regarded as conducive to certain characteristics of foreign policy behaviour and should be therefore used as the basis for the classification of such behaviour. He proposed three such attributes of states as being impressionistically the most important ones: geography and physical resources (large and small), state of economy (developed and underdeveloped), and state of polity (open and closed). This classification was widely discussed, criticized, refined, and applied for a number of years without producing satisfactory results. No reasonable empirical indicators could be agreed upon; several tests in applying the three attributes to the analysis of the behaviour of states showed that, with the exception of 'size', the attributes either singly or in combinations had no significant influence, but no new attributes have been thought of as being more significant.

After more than a decade of analysis of the attributes of states attempts at their better classification have not advanced much beyond the old-fashioned one into Great, Middle, and Small Powers, although post-1945 events have created the additional category of the Superpowers and arguably also one of the smallest units, 'microstates'. All these categories are based on various combinations of power and status, on which more in Chapter 7. There is no general agreement on the criteria and hence there is a considerable amount of confusion about the boundaries of each class. There is, nevertheless, also a considerable amount of agreement. Nobody would disagree with the contention that, say, the Maldive Islands are a very small, or micro- state and that a state like Brazil is not a small state, although they may disagree whether it is a Middle or a Great Power, as this depends on the nature of the definition. All agree that the United States and the Soviet Union should be singled out as two Superpowers and the vast majority limit this category to these two states.

The most realistic model seems to consist of a spectrum of states based upon power and status, with the two Superpowers at the one extreme and microstates at the other, leaving open the question where precisely an individual state may fit in between but recognizing that it is possible to agree about broad outlines of the zone of the spectrum into which it would fit, and often about ranking; thus Brazil is clearly closer to the 'Superpower' role than a small Central American Republic. It does not seem to be worthwhile to break up this spectrum into clearly-cut classes and impossible to illustrate them with the analysis of a representative state as none could be considered as really typical for a class. Chapter 5 on decision-making will therefore be devoted to the general categories useful in the analysis. The way to tackle the analysis of the substance of foreign policies will be indicated only by the subsequent example of the two Superpowers and China. Although by no means fully characteristic of other states, these are, of course, especially important in themselves. The two Superpowers not only pursue national foreign policies, as other states do, but also fulfil an important, some would say central, role in the functioning of the international system, while China is by far the most populous state on earth and the most likely runner-up to the Superpower status.

There is no general agreement about the most suitable framework for the analysis and comparison of foreign policies, although a fair degree of agreement exists about what are likely to be the most significant factors. A strong argument can be made in favour of an explicit scheme and hence one is offered here, without claiming special theoretical virtues for it. The significant factors are arranged in five groups:

1. Capabilities and salient characteristics, especially those deriving from geography and from historical tradition
2. Major features of the decision-making machinery
3. Major issues of foreign policy and the means to meet commitments
4. Attitudes to the most important states and blocs
5. Attitudes to international order.

Brief outlines of the policies of the two Superpowers and China are arranged according to this scheme.

The United States

1. The United States has a territory of over three million square miles and in the late seventies its population was reaching 220 million. In so far as they reflect isolation from Europe, American traditions resemble those of the British. Protected by the whole width of the Atlantic which was under the control of the benevolent British Navy, throughout the nineteenth century the Americans practised 'splendid isolation' and concentrated upon their continent. They conquered and colonized a large part of it, pushed forward 'the frontier of civilization', and evolved the 'Monroe Doctrine' which aimed at the exclusion of rivals from the remainder. They rapidly developed the great natural riches of their country and built up an industry on a scale hitherto unequalled.

The Americans had only one outside interest—to avoid an imperious incursion from Europe. Here they relied upon Britain to maintain the balance of power and to prevent the rise of a dangerous imperialist state in Europe. Consequently they had scarcely any foreign policy at all and their traditions in this field are extremely new. This preoccupation with domestic and continental affairs engendered the American conviction that the domestic and foreign spheres could be permanently separated, and also what some writers call 'the myth of omnipotence'—the belief that the unparalleled American domestic successes could be repeated also in international relations.

At the turn of the century the United States embarked on a policy of territorial expansion in the Pacific and the Far East. Its aims were not very clear; by and large they were to keep China independent—as a counterbalance to the rising might of Japan, and open—as a market for American trade.

The great open spaces of North America were almost empty and required labour for their development. First, slaves were imported from Africa; their emancipated descendants amount to over ten per cent of the American population today and, owing to the racial difference, have not been effectively assimilated. Then millions of European immigrants of various nationalities flocked into the United States. Thus, in complete contrast to the fairly homogeneous states of Western Europe, American society incorporated many different elements in quite recent times. The original common mould was largely shaped by British traditions, but the vast spaces, the persistence of the individual identities of the separate colonies, and the 'melting pot' of the various national and racial strains, produced a highly decentralized system characterized by a federal constitution, by lack of discipline within the two great national political parties, and by the prevalence of regional and particular interests. It is not only political power that is decentralized; there are also no national mass media, excepting the syndicated columns in the press and the occasional national hook-ups of television networks. In the sixties, the political system entered a period of crisis. The racial problems became increasingly acute and public opinion split over the American involvement in Vietnam; urban violence increased, culminating in recurrent summer riots and in the assassinations of one President and one Presidential candidate. In the next decade this was followed by the Watergate affair, a political scandal which forced President Richard Nixon to resign. By the end of the seventies, however, the American political system regained its stability. Its most acute and unresolved problems were economic—how to cope with the chronic weakness of the dollar induced mainly by large foreign trade deficits due to the massive imports of oil, the price of which quadrupled in 1973.

The basis of United States' power lies in its great natural resources, in its industrial system which, by any criteria, is the most evolved in the world, in its lead in technological advance, and in its unparalleled standards of living. In 1977, its population was 218·5 million, its G.N.P. was estimated at nearly $1,900 billion, of which six per cent was spent on defence. The United States continued to enjoy one of the highest *per capita* incomes in the world. During the seventies the effects of Vietnam and Watergate were to weaken presidential authority and the political will of the United States to match Soviet armament efforts and to oppose Soviet expansionist moves in Africa, but towards the end of the decade the trend seemed to have been reversed.

2. The nature of American democracy, particularly decentralization, the division of constitutional powers, and the impact of public opinion, are gravely prejudicial to an efficient foreign policy. De Tocqueville's famous remarks made over a century ago are still fully pertinent:

Foreign politics demand scarcely any of these qualities which are peculiar to democracy; they require, on the contrary, the perfect use of almost all those in which it is deficient . . . a democracy can only with great difficulties regulate the details of an important undertaking, persevere in a fixed design, and work out its execution in spite of serious obstacles. It cannot combine its measures with secrecy or await their consequences with patience.

American governmental machinery is extremely cumbersome. The President is undoubtedly the chief decision-maker within the Executive, but under him some fifty agencies deal with foreign affairs. The Congress, which, on the basis of the 'checks and balances' doctrine, has co-ordinate powers, interferes and, in the absence of party discipline, the President cannot control the regional and the sectional interests within it. Moreover, as national congressional elections take place every two years, the opinions of the electorate at large incessantly intrude.

Until 1945 American diplomacy was relatively undeveloped

and suffered from inadequate apparatus and insufficient profes-
sionalism; it was ill-equipped to cope with the difficult post-war
tasks. Since then the Americans have built up the largest diplomatic service on earth with missions in nearly all other states. This
service lacks long tradition and is gravely handicapped by the
activities of poorly co-ordinated intelligence and, to a lesser extent,
also aid-giving agencies, as well as by the constant intrusion of
domestic politics. However, its shortcomings and occasional blun-
ders must be viewed against the background of a generally successful development.

3. Within the first half of this century the Americans, who
formerly had little or no foreign policy, suddenly became one of the
two Superpowers, and their world-wide commitments required
from them a complete mental reorientation. In spite of occasional
disturbance, on the whole they were successful in their adjustments. When their security was menaced by the prospect of a
German victory, they reluctantly took part in the First World War;
equally unwillingly they entered the Second World War in 1941;
but in both wars they fought with will and determination. When
Britain was unable to continue her task of containing Communism, the United States stepped in in March 1947 with the
'Truman Doctrine', and became the protagonist in the 'cold war'.
With the Marshall Plan and NATO it stabilized the situation in
Europe, but its interventions in Asia were less uniformly successful. The Americans enabled Japan to rehabilitate herself and
prosper, and also Taiwan and South Korea, but were unsuccessful
in their attempts to ward off the establishment of a Communist
regime in China, and they then became involved in a prolonged
massive military intervention in Vietnam which was extremely
costly in terms of manpower and economic losses, as well as of
opprobrium at home and abroad.

Undoubtedly the major issues of United States foreign policy
today—military, political, economic, and ideological—all stem
from its position as a Superpower balancing the power of the Soviet
Union. American foreign policy requires great expenditure of
money, constant vigilance, and alert diplomacy. The Americans
have scored successes but have also suffered defeats, and the
clashing demands of their world-wide commitments often confront
them with apparently insoluble dilemmas. United States expendi-

ture on defence and other purposes of foreign policy was steadily mounting, especially during the intervention in Vietnam, but its rich economy could sustain it. During the seventies the effects of Vietnam and Watergate were to weaken presidential authority and the political will of the United States to match Soviet armament efforts, and to oppose Soviet expansionist moves in Africa, but towards the end of the decade the trend seemed to have been reversed.

In the order of their historical evolution, the major direct American foreign policy interests lie in the Western Hemisphere; the somewhat less direct interest in Europe is of equal age, whereas interest in Asia stems from the end of the last century only. The direct interest in the Western Hemisphere persists but, with the rapid growth in the population centres on the Pacific seaboard and of the importance of Japan and China, Asia and the Pacific have become rivals to Europe and the North Atlantic.

4. Ever since its rise to the position of a Superpower, the United States' foreign relations with the Soviet Union, its fellow Superpower, have become outstandingly important, including, as they do, the element of nuclear rivalry. In the 'cold war', the main objective of the United States was to deter a direct nuclear attack on the territory of the United States or its allies, and to contain Communist expansion, the danger of which had gradually spread from Europe and the Far East to all other continents and regions. In spite of the loose proclamation of a more active policy of 'liberation' in 1952, the American attitude to the Soviet Union remained fundamentally passive, as expressed in the formula of 'containment', coined by the influential diplomat, George F. Kennan. The United States pursued this policy by accumulating massive armaments, by concluding a series of alliances, and by establishing foreign bases. It furnished lavish aid, military and economic, to its allies and also to neutrals. The Communists scored a victory in China in 1949 but elsewhere the Americans succeeded in containing them—in Korea through a full-scale war fought with conventional weapons. Only in Vietnam were they unsuccessful, despite their large-scale involvement.

Stalin's death in 1953 ended the era of crude Soviet military menace. Thereafter the conflict began to shift to economic and ideological competition to win the sympathy of the non-committed, neutral states of Asia and Africa. Gradually the two Superpowers began to find accommodation on several important issues, including those of nuclear strategy and some of their respective spheres of interest. After having been brought to the brink of a direct clash during the Cuban Missile Crisis in October 1962, the 'cold war' gradually changed into what the Americans usually call a 'detente' and the Russians 'peaceful coexistence'. Tensions continued and the Soviet military intervention in Czechoslovakia in August 1968 disrupted progress. At the beginning of the seventies, serious new attempts started to limit the nuclear armaments race, leading to the partially successful Strategic Arms Limitations Talks (SALT), and the more successful stabilization of the division of Germany and of the status of Berlin. Detente did not, however, become firmly established and its probable peak, the Helsinki Conference on European Security and Co-operation in 1975, led not only to vastly increased economic exchanges but also to acrimonious disputes about human rights while the security results were not very promising, especially as the Russians were rapidly improving their armaments.

American relations with China were much slower to improve. After a direct armed clash in Korea, the Americans remained entrenched in their bases on Okinawa and on Taiwan, and became gradually involved in a massive military intervention in support of the anti-Communist regime in South Vietnam. Chinese success in developing nuclear weapons exacerbated the antagonism. A detente with China followed, however, the gradual American withdrawal from Vietnam in 1970 and 1971 and was firmly established by President Nixon's visit to Peking in February 1972. The Americans did not fully meet the Chinese desire to secure support against the Soviet Union to which they had become increasingly hostile. The issue of the continuing American support and recognition of Taiwan delayed the re-establishment of full diplomatic relations, but, following the death of Mao Tse-tung in 1975, relations between the two countries began to improve quite steadily.

American relations with other regions and states were to a very large extent a reflection of their relations with the Communist Powers; sometimes, to the detriment of American interests, they were excessively governed rather by the dictates of the 'cold war'. This applied even to allies: in the Western Hemisphere the Americans were unavailingly trying to transform the Organization of American States into an effective anti-Communist alliance, but, since 1961, they were compelled to endure the pro-Communist Government of Fidel Castro in Cuba; even their most successful coalition, the North Atlantic Treaty Organization, lost much of its urgency of purpose and proved incapable of resolving several serious problems of co-operation.

In the seventies the focus of immediate American concern shifted from security to economics. The security problems remained alive, although in a stabilized form, and security-oriented links survived, but an increasing proportion of American diplomatic effort went into the economic co-operation. This shift of emphasis was particularly pronounced in Asia. Whereas, in the immediate post-war years policy was based upon the 'containment' of Communism, first in and then outside China, culminating in the involvement in Vietnam, Japan, which by the end of the seventies had become the third-largest national economy in the world, became, with the E.E.C., the most important trade partner of the United States. Thus, while the security links with Japan and also South Korea, the Philippines, and Taiwan merely remained in force, diplomacy shifted to the problems of the consistent trade imbalance with Japan. Chastised by the experiences in Asia in the late seventies, the United States refrained from direct intervention in Africa to the point of being unwilling to counter widespread Soviet intervention which consisted of lavish military aid and of the use of Cuban forces.

5. Through traditions held in common with Britain, the Americans felt identified with the international order of the nineteenth century more than any other non-European state. They contributed to the evolution of some international norms, especially to the law of neutrality; throughout their early history, although concerned mainly with their own continent and foreign policy of 'isolationism', they remained intensely interested in the maintenance of the balance of power in Europe even though they did not experience the need to play an active part in it. When the balance was seriously threatened by the Germans in the two World Wars and by the Russians since, reluctantly but effectively they stepped into the breach.

The American attitude to a new international order embodied in the international institutions of the twentieth century was inconsistent. Although the League of Nations was President Wilson's brain-child, American public opinion did not share his internationalism and the Senate refused to ratify the Peace Treaty of Versailles and to join the Organization. During the Second World War, the Americans were determined to set up a new order and were the initiators and main proponents of the United Nations as the comprehensive institution as well as of the important Specialized Agencies dealing with economics. This was the manifestation both of their conviction that this would be in their own national interest as well as of their idealistic convictions. Indeed, at first, the United Nations could be regarded as an instrument of imposing a *pax Americana* upon the world: with the support of the Latin American states (twenty out of the original membership of fifty) and of the Western European allies, the Americans commanded crushing anti-Russian majorities on all controversial matters which came up before the General Assembly. They greatly benefited from the United Nations' sponsorship of what was in fact an American intervention in Korea. But even in the sixties and seventies, after the easy majorities had disappeared in a membership which had nearly tripled, the Americans retained a positive attitude to the Organization and remained the most generous contributor to its finances. Being located in New York and thus providing local news, the United Nations figured in the American mass media much more frequently than in those of any other country. In the late seventies, however, tensions arising from the new minority position and from the violently anti-Israeli and anti-capitalist policies of the majorities began to tell, resulting in the withdrawal of the United States from the membership of the International Labour Organization (I.L.O.) and in threats of withdrawal from the United Nations Educational, Scientific, and Cultural Organization (UNESCO).

It may be added that these ecumenical ideas did not fully eliminate all narrower ideas of an international order. The Americans have officially abandoned the traditional Monroe Doctrine, embodying their aspiration to control the Western Hemisphere, and it is increasingly unlikely that they would resort to another direct military intervention, the last of which occurred as late as 1965 in the Dominican Republic. They retain, however, a primary interest in maintaining order within the region which means excluding the rise of Communist regimes, although tolerating Castro's on Cuba, after attempts to remove it had failed. They extended this notion of a regional order to what they sometimes called 'the free world', meaning all anti-Communist countries, which, at least theoretically, subscribed to the ideas of liberal democracy and free market economy. Again, theoretically, it is conceivable that—in concert with the Soviet Union—the United States could introduce a world-order based on the drawing of boundaries between their respective spheres of interests. Such an order is unlikely. The Communist world is split; Communist expansion into the Western Hemisphere militates against such accommodation; moreover, the Americans feel a fundamental antagonism to Communism and could not accept Communist rule over a third of mankind even as a factor of stability.

The Soviet Union

1. Any analysis of Soviet affairs must inevitably include a discussion of Communist ideology. All countries are governed by systems of values and beliefs which we now call ideologies, but, whereas in the United States or in any other established non-Communist country ideologies have organically developed together with other political and social traditions, in the Soviet Union the Communist ideology was imposed upon the country in 1917 and its exact relation to the Tsarist heritage is still disputed.

Although most Marxists emphatically deny that the geographical position of a country may have a determining effect on its foreign policy, this is more clearly the case with Russia than with many other countries. Russia is by far the largest state on earth, embracing over 8½ million square miles, fully one-half of the Eurasian continent. No 'natural frontiers' exist to which Russia could aspire since no physical features delimit her from the Central European plain. The country is clearly indefensible, and the fluctuating nature of Russian frontiers reflects the strength or weakness of the central government. For three centuries Russia was under the Tartar yoke and as late as in the seventeenth century she had temporarily a Polish ruler.

While the indeterminate nature of Russian frontiers made the country an easy prey for attacks, it also encouraged the Russians to seek security through expansion. They expanded in all directions, reaching the physical limits of the Arctic and Pacific Oceans and clashing with neighbouring countries everywhere else. In contrast to the relative isolation of the United States, Russia was in constant interaction with her neighbours—when she was weak and disunited she was subject to depredations, while, when strong and united, she expanded as far as possible. The traditional aims of Russian foreign policy are to absorb or truncate weak neighbours and to exercise as much control as possible over those unwilling to yield and able to resist. Her specific territorial objectives are sea-outlets, ice-free ports, the subject of the historical drives towards the Straits, the Gulf, and the Yellow Sea.

The imperious demands of foreign policy set such a premium upon unity and centralization that Russia achieved a fair degree of both despite her enormous area and her large population divided into some 150 ethnic and linguistic groups which differ greatly in many important characteristics. Although her constitution is federal in form, the Soviet Union perpetuates the Tsarist tradition of central control which is now exercised by the Communist Party.

The October Revolution in 1917 brought into power the Bolsheviks whose Marxist ideology not only prescribed a new leading objective of world revolution but also a new system of knowledge and new strategies of foreign policy. During the twenties the break with the past seemed to be complete: the Soviet rulers were pursuing their goal of world revolution in a ruthless and unprecedented fashion. When, however, in the late twenties this goal was replaced by that of 'building socialism in one country', and when various traditional Russian policies and ways of behaviour were revived, the question of the interrelation between ideology and national tradition began to loom large. While some Western experts contend that Soviet foreign policy is still rigidly controlled by ideology, others claim that this is merely a thin disguise for traditional Tsarist policies which are no more than the obvious reaction to the challenges arising in Russia's environment. Others again try to combine both approaches and to study the changes in ideology in actual Soviet practice.

The Soviet regime successfully controlled the country and industrialized it, won the Second World War and recovered from its colossal destruction, but only through the exercise of a strict and ruthless totalitarian regime, oppressive to the citizens. By the end of the Second World War, the Union secured the position of a Superpower. The problem of her nationalities remained, however, unresolved, and, especially from the death of Stalin in 1953, the Soviet rulers have been facing increasingly insistent demands for greater political liberty and more consumer goods.

The Soviet Union possesses tremendous natural resources, but an unevenly developed industrial system. Although in some respects her rockets and some of her heavy armaments surpass in their sophistication those manufactured in the United States, she is quite backward in most branches of consumer goods and she cannot master the organization of agriculture in which collective and state farms have proved quite inadequate. In 1977, the population of the Soviet Union was 258 million; after a period of very rapid post-war economic growth which slowed down in the seventies, her G.N.P. did not reach $420 billion and of this some 11–13 per cent was spent on defence. Consequently her per capita income remained low, when compared with that of the United States.[1]

2. As in all single-party authoritarian states, the making of foreign policy in the Soviet Union is characterized by complete control by the Communist Party of the Soviet Union (C.P.S.U.). The governmental apparatus, including the Foreign Ministry, is a mere executant of the policies decided by it. Within the Party, power was formerly rigidly concentrated in the hands of Stalin but, under the 'collective leadership' which succeeded him, it was vested in the Praesidium or Politburo numbering eleven to fifteen. Between 1956 and 1963 the First Secretary of the Party, Nikita Khrushchev, dominated Soviet politics and was internationally the only prominent figure, but he was not a dictator with unlimited powers; he depended upon the other members of the Praesidium, and also, to a much smaller extent, on the members of the larger Central Committee of the Party. Since the removal of Khrushchev no individual has become fully predominant in Soviet leadership, including the long-lasting Leonid Brezhnev.

Soviet diplomacy is unorthodox; it engages in widespread

---

[1] Soviet statistics are not fully comparable with Western statistics and the data are unreliable.

espionage and propaganda and is therefore generally distrusted. Moreover, it is rigid and is slavishly dependent upon central orders. Consequently, in spite of the large funds at its disposal and the great pool of ability from which it can draw, it is not particularly successful. There are no signs that the position has changed since Stalin's death; the blundering treatment of the Czechoslovak crisis in 1968, and of the human rights issue after 1975, indicate that it is essentially similar.

3. Soviet foreign policy cannot be evaluated with any degree of certainty because we cannot be sure to which of their objectives the Russians give priority; in fact the Russian leaders themselves are divided, or unclear, or both. The Soviet Union is a rapidly developing country in which the standard of living of the citizens is still very low. Although it is working at full strength and is still expanding, the Soviet economy cannot provide enough for the growing needs of consumption, the mounting military expenditure, and foreign aid. In the sixties and, even more so, when economic growth slowed down in the late seventies, it was becoming obvious that, although in possession of all the elements of power, the Soviet Union was feeling the strain rather acutely.

It is not a case of the proverbial choice between guns and butter; all Soviet rulers chose and are likely to go on choosing guns as long as they deem these essential for national security. The question now is to what extent they feel that they must continuously work with all the means at their disposal for a world revolution which, according to the Marxist doctrine, is anyway inevitable. Even if this goal retains its high value, they may now have more efficient means to increase their power through further economic development at home rather than through political and military expansion. Moreover, having already secured a fairly high level of industrial and social advancement, they are likely to be chary of risking their achievements through foreign adventures, and this advancement may have, to some extent, transformed their ideology. Finally, although at the moment this is highly speculative, in view of the difficulties arising from their relations with Communist China, the Russians may find the prospect of an all-Communist world much less attractive; in some respects their interests seem to coincide with those of the capitalist highly-industrialized countries of the North and of the white race.

These are, of course, Western interpretations of the major issues of Soviet foreign policy. It is quite likely that many, perhaps most of the Soviet leaders genuinely believe their own protestations that Soviet foreign policy is defensive, that the Soviet Union is threatened from all directions by the United States which has established a ring of alliances and military bases all around the Union, and which conducts a strongly anti-Communist policy. The future development of Soviet foreign policy is bound to revolve around these two fundamental issues: priority of domestic or foreign commitments, and evaluation of American intentions.

4. Thus, clearly Soviet relations with the United States dominate the whole of Soviet foreign policy. It is difficult to appreciate from the outside what the Russians exactly mean by their slogan of 'peaceful coexistence' with the capitalist world. Although crude military expansionism ceased with Stalin's death, a fundamental hostility and distrust persists. In all probability, many Soviet Communists still think in terms of the ultimately inevitable war between the United States and the Soviet Union. Even Khrushchev, the main architect of peaceful coexistence, repeatedly made it clear that it meant to him not the abandonment of hostility but merely a shift of the conflict from the military to other fields. To some extent, Soviet-American relations are bound to depend on what the Americans do and on how they behave but, in all likelihood, they depend very much more on the evolution of Soviet society and of Communist ideology.

Soviet relations with other Communist states give rise to problems which are much more complex and independent of the cold war than similar problems confronting the United States in relations with its allies. Until 1945 these countries had not been either Communist or under Russian rule. In conformity both with Tsarist tradition and with the goal of a world revolution, the Soviet Union imposed Communist regimes wherever the Red Army marched: local Communists seized power by themselves only in Yugoslavia and later also in China. It was difficult for the Soviet Union to control the new Communist governments as they had habitually done with Communist parties abroad: in 1947–8 they tried in vain to squash nationalist opposition in Yugoslavia; in 1956 Poland and Hungary asserted their individualities.

Of greatest importance, however, was the Sino-Soviet rift which came out into the open in the late fifties and gradually grew until China became a dangerous and outspoken opponent of the Soviet Union, threatening her long frontier by her claims for the return of lost territories, rivalling her as a more radical leader of international Communism, admittedly with only limited success. In the late sixties, the Communist bloc further loosened, with Albania coming out firmly on the side of China, with Rumania asserting herself through an independent foreign policy, and, in 1968, through Czechoslovakia rapidly liberalizing her regime. With the assistance of similarly apprehensive regimes in Eastern Germany, Poland, Hungary, and Bulgaria, the Russians first threatened the liberalizers and then had to resort to a large-scale military intervention in Czechoslovakia, showing how brittle the solidarity of the bloc had become. Patriotism united the Czechs and the Slovaks against the occupiers. In the late seventies the 'Euro-Communism' of the Western Communist countries went out of control. Instead of being monolithic, the Communist bloc is now clearly polycentric; the various Communist governments and parties are dependent on the Soviet Union militarily and economically and cannot effectively defend themselves. Nevertheless, they are able to exercise a fair degree of independence, according to their individual strength and determination.

In their relations with the non-committed countries, the Soviet leaders came up against a contradiction between their support for world revolution and for foreign Communists and their interest in alignment with 'bourgeois-nationalist' governments which were willing to stay out of American alliances. They were inconsistent and vacillating. After initial opposition to the new governments, they unsuccessfully attempted to cajole them into an anti-Western 'camp of peace' which would embrace the Communist and the non-committed blocs. In the early sixties they abandoned this policy as unpromising. At first, the Russians scored diplomatic successes in Asia, Africa, and Latin America owing to two important assets which were effective in spite of their contradictory diplomacy: the imperialist taint of the Western Powers and the prestige of the Communist formula for 'pulling oneself up by one's own boot straps', of economic growth through central planning. Although the continuing racial problems in Southern Africa tended to ensure sympathy with Communism among the Africans, by the late seventies the Western imperialist excesses and exploitation were otherwise a matter of the past and the Russian model of economic growth had become tarnished by its shortcomings everywhere it had been applied and even in the Soviet Union itself. Furthermore, for some time the Russians had been suffering from Chinese competition, both in ideology and aid-giving and, moreover, could scarcely afford substantial economic aid, except to a few selected countries. When, however, new opportunities for intervention in Africa appeared in the late seventies as a result of inter-African struggles, the Russians intervened in great strength both in Angola and on the Horn of Africa.

5. Although in many respects the Soviet rulers have reverted to Tsarist traditions, it was obviously impossible for them to build upon the traditional Russian attitudes to international order. As one of the major Powers, the Tsarist regime had participated in the Concert of Europe and even wished to transform it into a kind of world government which would intervene whenever necessary to preserve the *status quo*. The Communist regime pursued a policy which was the very opposite of this: instead of being whole-heartedly conservative, it was revolutionary; instead of wishing to preserve the existing order, it aimed at its complete overthrow. As long as the final goal of world revolution persists, and the Soviet rulers cannot abandon it because it is the crux of their ideological legitimacy both at home and among Communist Parties abroad, they cannot take part in international transactions on the same footing as other, non-revolutionary states. They reject the existing order as undesirable and untenable, even if possibly they no longer consider the task of abolishing it as very urgent or even desirable. 'Peaceful coexistence' with non-Communist states is merely tactics, though probably quite long-range tactics.

Soviet attitudes to the institutions serving international order shape accordingly. The Russian leaders believe in one type of internationalism alone—the proletarian, through the solidarity of the working classes with the Communist governments. Their relations with non-Communist governments are fundamentally inimical if not actively hostile. Their diplomacy is less a way of arriving at an agreement with other states than a method of conducting hostile propaganda. To them, international law which expresses and buttresses the existing order is as undesirable as the order itself; international institutions are controlled by and serve the ends of capitalist states.

All these declared attitudes and intentions certainly do not represent a faithful picture of Soviet diplomatic practice which frequently deviates from them and increasingly resembles the orthodox diplomacy of Western Powers. Thus, when interested in the conclusion of a specific treaty, the Russians stress their habit of faithful adherence to agreements: in the mid-thirties, when afraid of Hitler, they tried to bring to life the moribund collective security system of the League; in 1950, when confronted with the United Nations' support for the American action in South Korea, they immediately resumed participation in the organs of the institution which they had been boycotting for several months; they began to represent themselves as defenders of the non-committed countries against imperialism and cashed in on their anti-colonial and hence anti-Western sentiments to harass the Western Powers in the General Assembly. At the same time, wishing to avoid the possibility of an independent, i.e. potentially anti-Communist activity, they tried to induce the neutrals to support the Soviet proposals for the splitting of the central position of the Secretary-General into a 'troika', a three-man directorate, one of whom would represent the uncommitted states, and thus paralyse the organization.

Until Stalin's death the fundamental hostility of the Soviet Union to the existing international order could not be doubted, but one cannot reject the possibility that the Soviet Union then began to shed her aggressively revolutionary character and is becoming more conservative, more ready to participate in the preservation of the existing order within which she has secured herself a leading position. She has to compete with Communist China and has much to lose in a general war; she also increasingly relies upon access to Western technology and credits and, on some North-South issues, finds common interests with other industrialized countries.

China

In the early post-war decades the Chinese variant of Communism was much more extreme and virulent than the Russian, partly because China's problems were more acute and her demands less satisfied, and partly because she was still in her early post-revolutionary stage—the Chinese Revolution was completed only in 1949, thirty-two years after the October Revolution in Russia. Nevertheless, since Russia and not China is the main champion of world revolution, and since the main Chinese ambitions are limited to Asia and co-terminous with the traditional sphere of interest and influence of the Chinese Empire, there can be no doubt about the significance of China's national traditions, which go back some 5,000 years.

Like Russia, China is predominantly a land-Power. Although she commands a long sea-coast, only during the period of the early Mings, about the time of the Tudors, did the Chinese develop a powerful ocean-going navy. In Chinese history the pendulum swings from integration into a loose imperial whole to disintegration into many provinces governed by warlords; recurrent barbarian invasions from Central Asia are followed by the absorption and assimilation of the invaders; dynasties follow one another—according to Chinese political theory each receives a mandate from heaven and retains it so long as it can cope with the tasks of government, but loses it if it fails. The Communist government can be understood as another dynastic government replacing its predecessor which lost its mandate from heaven, but a government with a difference. It has introduced some European technology and Communist political and industrial techniques into a hitherto oriental background.

China with her more than 4½ million square miles ranks among the largest states on earth although she is much smaller than the Soviet Union. Nevertheless her population, by far the largest of any single state, uncomfortably crowds the area. According to not very reliable statistics, the population in 1977 probably surpassed 900 million. Food-production in China depends upon colossal irrigation works for which the central government has always been responsible, and the totalitarian Communist society perpetuates and develops the tradition of the 'hydraulic' society of China.

Tremendous distances and poor communications obstructed full political integration, which the Chinese achieved only a few times and for brief periods. Nevertheless, they developed a strong cultural unity and managed to assimilate the invading barbarians and some non-Chinese border-people. They gradually spread their influence in the neighbouring countries; the 'Kingdom of the

Middle' became the centre of a vast political system with vassals and satellites and tribute-payers in various degrees of dependence. Throughout history Chinese borders have violently fluctuated and shifted, so that modern China can claim territories which had once been Chinese from every single one of her neighbours.

During its short period in power, the Communist regime has not only mobilized the population politically and economically in an unprecedented fashion but has endeavoured to maintain the momentum of the 'permanent revolution' through a series of upheavals, although only at the cost of increasingly grave crises. The last one of these, the 'Cultural Revolution', which began in 1966, led to prolonged factional fighting which paralysed China's educational system and gravely disturbed her industrial production. Only by 1970 did the movement subside. The death in 1976 of Mao Tse-Tung, the founder and leader of the Republic, resulted in a brief struggle for succession followed by the establishment of an apparently stable and moderate leadership.

The economic basis of China's power is uncertain. The country commands considerable mineral resources but not many of them have been explored and even fewer are being fully exploited. China's industrial development on any scale started only under the Communist regime, but was disrupted when Soviet aid was stopped, and then by the repeated upheavals and by the struggle for Mao's succession. It lags far behind that of the Soviet Union. The Chinese have managed to develop thermo-nuclear technology and some heavy industry but these are uncharacteristic; China remains a predominantly peasant society. No reliable statistics are available about her economy but it seems clear that her G.N.P. and her *per capita* income have remained extremely low and that her defence expenditure is proportionately high but insufficient for modernized military equipment.

2. The institutions of Communist China have been moulded on those of the Soviet Union, but China, being nationally nearly homogeneous, did not employ the federal form. As in the Soviet Union, the Communist Party is supreme, but it had a somewhat different history: it never went through a period of one-person dictatorship quite as monolithic as that of Stalin. Scarcely a decade after the final success of the Revolution, the Chinese Party leadership split on lines very similar to those observable in the Soviet

Union; the radical wing was probably more powerful and controlled policy. The split became increasingly acute, eventually leading to a sustained but unsuccessful attempt by Chairman Mao to reimpose his control through the 'Cultural Revolution'. The radical leadership retrospectively called 'the Gang of Four' became increasingly dominant in Mao's last years but soon after his death it was replaced by a more moderate leadership.

3. Compared with the Soviet Union, China has little reason to be satisfied with the *status quo*. The Chinese are poverty-stricken, and, despite their enormous efforts under Communist leadership, they have made little progress towards industrialization. Moreover, they advance several territorial claims based upon national security and upon historical rights—notably their claim for the incorporation of Taiwan, at present under the control of the rival Nationalist Government, which enjoys the support of the United States, for a number of islands in the surrounding seas and, probably most importantly although rather vaguely, for the revision of their long boundary with the Soviet Union.

Relief of poverty is undoubtedly the most urgent of governmental tasks, and the Chinese are under much greater pressure than the Russians to give priority to requirements of economic growth over those of foreign policy. The leadership, however, seemed to have been governed ever since 1949 primarily by political considerations. Their foreign policy can be explained by an apprehension over China's security, understandable in the light of the encroachments upon her territory by the Russians from the land in the nineteenth century, and by the Westerners and Japan from the sea towards its end and early in the twentieth century. It can, however, also be attributed to considerations of Communist ideology and to an aspiration to restore the old imperial frontiers and spheres of influence. Only following the conclusion of the succession struggles after Mao's death did Chinese leadership turn decisively towards economic priorities, seeking a much greater pace of economic development.

4. The tradition of being self-centred and the absence of adequate capabilities for a world role combine to restrict China to a more pronouncedly regional sphere of operations than those of the previously discussed Superpowers. Her long-lasting antagonism to the United States was based fundamentally on Asian politics.

The Chinese were slow to forget the United States' support for the Nationalists during the Civil War and now on Taiwan, and the interventions in Korea and in Vietnam, close to Chinese borders. The conflict includes an ideological element and is usually presented by the Chinese in an ideological garb but it can be equally well interpreted as being purely power political. This is confirmed by the seemingly decisive way in which the Chinese turned to the United States during the seventies in order to counterbalance the Soviet Union which they began to perceive as their main threat.

The basic importance of China's relations with the Soviet Union is much greater as they share a land-frontier 4,300 miles long. Despite the common Communist ideology and the common hostility to the United States, this relationship was far from easy. The Russians only reluctantly restored to China their Manchurian concessions and gave her inadequate economic aid. An open rift arose in the later fifties and has become exacerbated since. The Chinese are unwilling to conform to the Soviet Union in their domestic or in their foreign policies. As the Russians withdrew aid facilities and refused to assist China in her nuclear programme, the Chinese became increasingly hostile, competing with the Russians for the leadership of world Communism and raising claims for the restoration of the territories forfeited to Russia in the nineteenth century. Massive formations of Russian troops with equipment much more modern than that of the Chinese army were massed along the frontier and Soviet nuclear missiles were facing Chinese territory. From 1969 recurrent armed clashes occurred on the disputed territories and, occasionally, the possibility of a Soviet nuclear attack or of an extensive conventional conflict seemed possible.

With her Asian neighbours and near-neighbours which once came within the orbit of the peripheries of her ancient empire, China occasionally revives her shadowy claims giving rise to a suspicion of an expansionist policy. These Asian countries are the major sphere of her operations also in her two attempts to play a world role—either as a leader of an anti-imperialist bloc or as a leader of the international Communist movement. In both guises China acted in opposition to the Soviet Union, first in endeavouring to befriend the anti-imperialist but non-Communist states, which culminated in the Bandung Conference in April 1955, while the Russians persisted in a rigid 'two-camps' doctrine; then in trying to obtain influence over the international Communist movement. Her outstanding problems were conflicts over the sovereignty of small islands with Taiwan, South Korea, Japan, and Vietnam which had suddenly become economically important as bases for the exploitation of fisheries and of the likely deposits of oil in the surrounding waters. In 1978 a more general conflict broke out with Vietnam, united under a Communist but fiercely independent national leadership.

Chinese forays outside Asia proved futile. Her influence over Albania, which is of marginal importance, lasted over a decade, her intercessions on behalf of Eastern European states in 1956 and 1968 were ineffective, and her influence in Cuba and in a few African states only ephemeral. China proved powerful on the battlefield when she held the United States to a stalemate in the Korean War in 1951 and when she scored decisive victories against India in 1962. She has by far the largest land-army on earth adequate to overwhelm any of her neighbours except the Soviet Union and perhaps India, but it is short of modern equipment and of logistic support. Moreover, China is highly deficient in capital and other resources for industrialization, and she clearly depends on extensive outside support. In the late seventies, having apparently firmly decided that the Soviet Union is the major adversary rather than a potential source of supply, the post-Mao leaders turned to the United States and the other industrialized countries for technological support both for industrialization and for modernization of the armed forces.

5. Logically, China's attitude to international order is more negative than Russia's. Her historical traditions are purely oriental and she tends to revert to the disdainful style of imperial diplomacy in which all other states were treated as barbarian and subordinate. Until the seventies her aims were pronouncedly revisionist and, unlike the Soviet Union, she had not had much opportunity or reason to demonstrate even a temporary and limited acceptance of international law or to join international institutions. China is a founder-member of the United Nations and one of the five Permanent Members of the Security Council, but until 1971 she was represented by the Nationalist Government of China whose rule is limited to Taiwan. As a result of American

pressures, the Communist Government was not only deprived of representation in the United Nations but was also branded by it as an aggressor in Korea and was subjected to United Nations sanctions.

The Chinese leaders have been using their representation in the United Nations and their renewed connections with the world, established in the seventies, mainly to counteract Soviet influence. There was no indication that their basic attitude to international order was becoming really positive and they did not participate in the international negotiations on nuclear weapons.

4 Non-state actors

The crisis of the territorial state

After the final consolidation of the major states in Europe in modern times, states were considered stable, permanent units. To contemporaries, the elimination of Venice during the Napoleonic Wars appeared to be daemonic; the disappearance of Poland as a result of three partitions at the end of the eighteenth century left an explosive issue of Polish restoration which repeatedly disturbed international relations; other cases were few and of little importance. The First World War shook this stability of states. It destroyed two large empires, the Austro-Hungarian and the Ottoman, and replaced them with a number of new states established on the principle of 'national self-determination' which was unattainable in the complex mixture of nationalities in Europe. The Second World War seemingly weakened stability even further. The two new Superpowers, the United States and the Soviet Union, which shouldered the primary responsibility for the stability of the international system, were both relatively inexperienced in diplomacy; all other nation-states emerged from the war in a really shattered condition. Moreover, soon there proliferated a multitude of new states arising from the break-up of colonial empires, which were largely inexperienced in the European traditions of international society and often unwilling to accept them.

In the first post-war decade the issue of the precarious nature of international stability was often conveniently summed up in terms of the 'viability' of states. According to the cogent analysis of John Herz,[1] we were facing a situation closely resembling that of the sixteenth and seventeenth centuries when the small medieval units were merging into modern states. As the gunpowder revolution had made the former inadequate for the needs of the day, so the technological revolution of the war and the post-war period rendered the territorial states obsolete. For some time the frontiers

[1] John Herz, *International Politics in the Nuclear Age*, 1959.

had been losing their meaning as lines delineating a territory under the complete sovereignty of its government. The first challenges were economic and psychological. Industrialized and hence no longer fully self-supporting states became extremely vulnerable to severance from external sources of supplies and markets. Psychological warfare was already in evidence during the French Revolution, and, during the Napoleonic wars, blockades proved quite effective. Then industrialization greatly increased economic vulnerability, and, after its invention, radio became extensively utilized for propaganda by all states. The main challenge, however, came from the recent technological developments in warfare, from the bombers, and, even more so, from the nuclear weapons and long-range ballistic missiles. The interior of the states, even of the Superpowers, suddenly became 'soft', since it could be effectively struck from the outside.

While the erosion of the impenetrability of states weakened the external roots of their sovereign existence, they became seriously threatened also by explosive domestic forces. In the post-war world they were called upon to satisfy a rapidly growing variety of social needs and demands at a time when their capacity to do so had been seriously diminished. Independently of the nature of the political and socio-economic regimes, all states faced the same fundamental problem of having turned into extremely complex multi-functional forms of social organization while becoming increasingly less capable of fulfilling all their functions: for security and for many major economic issues, they were too small but, at the same time, for a variety of domestic issues, they were much too big, as the citizens, especially some minorities, violently objected to the lack of grass roots influence on national policies. Thus states in their traditional form faced disruptive forces from two directions: defence and some major economic needs called for merger in larger units whereas dissatisfactions at home required greater pluralism, recognition of the interests of groups, the grant of autonomous powers below governmental levels, and, in the case of really dissatisfied national minorities, even the separation and the break-up of the traditional units. The two groups of demands were often incompatible; both threatened the very continuation of states.

Nevertheless, the survival powers of states have proved to be unexpectedly great. By the end of the seventies, when the scattered residual remains of colonial empires were still achieving statehood and adding new, ostensibly even less 'viable' new members to the family of nations, no cases of disintegration or disappearance of a legitimate state had been recorded. It requires a longer historical perspective to arrive at a balanced assessment of the causes for the tough durability of states, and no explanation can be offered here; some likely major factors are listed below but they clearly do not apply to all cases and do not add up to more than a fairly impressionistic checklist:

1. States generally retain their legitimacy, both domestically and internationally.

2. They remain the largest-scale meaningful communities and command the supreme loyalty of the vast majority of their citizens, particularly as political representatives of nations and as guardians of national cultures.

3. They retain the monopoly of territory and the near-monopoly of large-scale legitimate force.

4. They remain the only truly comprehensive large-scale multi-functional organizations with great built-in powers of inertia due to the variety of the social needs for which they cater, and to the built-in bureaucratic and other sectional interests which have a stake in their survival.

5. Negatively, they have not been generally faced with really serious rivals.

6. Perhaps most importantly, as the discontinuation of any state could undermine the stability of the international system as a whole and threaten others with a possibility of a major war, disastrous to all, everybody has now a substantial stake in the continuation of the *status quo*.

At the same time, however, the membership of the international system is decisively broadening beyond states alone, although the latter have, at least so far, retained their dominant position. In order to meet the new challenges they have developed new institutional devices—coalitions, blocs, international organizations. In one way all these serve the purpose of buttressing the sovereignty of their members; but in another, they are further undermining it by becoming actors in international society in their own right and by pursuing their own interests or those of international society as a whole, as distinct from the individual interests of their members.

Interstate governmental organizations

There are three main types of these new groupings of states—regional, functional, and comprehensive. The regional groupings are of shorter standing but became conspicuous in the post-war years when the Communist and the anti-Communist blocs gave the appearance of developing into two rival empires which would eventually divide the whole globe. Although the bipolarization did not fully materialize, institutions of great moment grew within the two blocs.

The North Atlantic Treaty Organization (NATO) is concerned with the defence of Western Europe and the Atlantic; it includes the United States, Canada, and their thirteen European allies. NATO constituted a departure from the traditional patterns of international military co-operation in that it was the first alliance to establish in peacetime a permanent integrated force under joint command. This force neatly solved the problem of German re-armament by including all the German forces and thus preventing the re-establishment of an exclusively national German force. Other members, however, retained some of their forces under their individual, national controls. Moreover, the strategic nuclear forces and the members' commitments outside Europe were excluded from the scope of NATO. Thus the Organization did not override the sovereignty of its members in defence matters though it circumscribed it to a considerable extent. The Supreme Commander of the integrated force, invariably an American, is in direct command of some of their troops and they are committed in advance to a range of strategic decisions. Moreover, the national defence programmes are negotiated with the Organization at an early stage of their formulation and come up for discussion at the North Atlantic Council in December each year, thus influencing their national parliaments. Finally, NATO serves the purpose of debate and adjustment of the foreign policies of its members towards the Soviet Union. Members do, however, often persist with their individual views and policies against NATO pressures;

the ultimate decision is theirs and NATO has no provision for majority voting.

The evolution of NATO was slow and uneasy. The members' dedication was directly related to their fears of the Soviet Union and therefore NATO thrived under the impact of the Korean crisis but began to wilt when the cold war abated. Its strategic provisions were never fully adequate for the defence of Europe, as its members did not provide the minimum forces necessary for this defence in a conventional war, whereas its place in the nuclear strategy became somewhat doubtful when the United States replaced its 'massive retaliation' doctrine by that of 'graduated deterrence'. There is no satisfactory doctrine for the employment of tactical nuclear weapons assigned to NATO by the United States and remaining under American control, and no institutional form has been found for incorporating a strategic nuclear component. Politically, NATO has managed to live with but not to resolve the problems of the preponderance of the United States within the Organization, to arbitrate in the feuds between individual members such as between Britain and Iceland over fisheries or between Greece and Turkey over Cyprus, to cope with the issues arising from the American, British, and French interests outside Europe, as manifested in the Suez Crisis in 1956 or on the Vietnam issue.

As the political detente between the Americans and the Russians was weakening the basis of the alliance, by the mid-sixties NATO entered a period of crisis which culminated in President de Gaulle's withdrawal in 1966 from all its military organs although not from the political alliance. NATO's original sense of purpose was, however, revived by the Soviet military intervention in Czechoslovakia in 1968 and by continuing Soviet incursions into the Middle East and Africa. The Organization survived the succession of internal crises due to technological developments, differences over strategy, and other issues among members, economic stringencies, and the continuing direct bilateral negotiations between the Americans and the Russians, the Strategic Arms Limitations Talks (SALT). A decade later, NATO had become consolidated again and showed signs of having assumed the character of a permanent actor in the international system.

The institutions of the European Communities, the European

Economic Community (the E.E.C. or the Common Market), the
European Coal and Steel Community (E.C.S.C.) and the
EURATOM are, in a way, even further-reaching. Their original
membership of six—France, the Federal Republic of Germany,
Italy, and the smaller Benelux countries (the Netherlands, Bel-
gium, and Luxembourg) was enlarged by the adhesion of Great
Britain, Denmark and Ireland in 1973; in the late seventies,
Greece, Portugal, and Spain were negotiating for their admission.

The Communities bear a 'supranational' character, which
means that, within their spheres of activities, they can actually
make decisions which are binding upon members. Their central
organs—now amalgamated—act on behalf of the Communities,
but must obtain for important decisions the concurrence of the
Council of Ministers, although within this Council not all decisions require unanimity. Consequently a member can be over-
ruled, can be obliged even unwillingly to pursue a policy decided
upon by the Community, although not on an issue it regards as
vital. Finally, in contrast to the customary time-limitation of
treaties or the provisions for withdrawal, after an initial brief
period, membership of the E.E.C. is permanent. The Communities are meant to be a step towards the political integration of
Western Europe, which, however, has not progressed very far in
other fields.

At first, the progress of the European Communities was slow
and halting. The E.C.S.C. was established in 1951 as an avowed
first step towards a European Federation, but its proposed successors, the European Defence and Political Communities, came to
grief by 1954. The favourable market conditions and the great
efforts of the dedicated European 'integrationists' were the only
reasons why the E.C.S.C. not only survived but was followed by
the establishment in 1957 of the other two Communities. The
Communities then went rapidly from strength to strength, attracting Britain and the other reluctant outsiders to make unsuccessful
attempts to join them. By the mid-sixties, however, they reached a
crisis. The boom was over and the economic growth slowed down;
the Communities became institutionally amalgamated but
increasingly cluttered up by their own bureaucracies. Most importantly, grave political difficulties arose between France and the
other members owing to de Gaulle's opposition to further progress

towards supranational controls as well as to accepting Britain as a member. Like NATO, the European Communities also reached a stage of acute crisis.

In the seventies these trends were reversed, although not very conspicuously or quite decisively. The expansion of membership strengthened the Communities politically but further obstructed their decision-making processes through introducing additional national interests and styles. At the same time, however, as the largest international trader, the E.E.C. began to play an increasing role in co-ordinating the members' international trade policies and, gradually, to some limited extent also, other foreign policies. Thus the E.E.C. spoke on behalf of its members in the G.A.T.T. (General Agreement on Trade and Tariffs) negotiations, and agricultural and fisheries policies and at the Helsinki Conference on European Security and Co-operation and its sequels. It fully co-ordinated its members' attitudes; it secured recognition and attracted diplomatic representation as an important international actor by the vast majority of states, including, after initial hesitation, also the Soviet Union.

After a series of unsuccessful attempts in 1978 the E.E.C. made another, more serious one in a move towards stabilizing E.E.C. currencies, and a form of democratic control was introduced by implementing a decision to elect the European Parliament directly. It was clear that the full political integration originally envisaged would not succeed in the face of the rooted attachment to the individual national interests, especially in France and Britain, but, also, that the Communities would be increasingly called upon to act on behalf of all their members whenever these would prove incapable of acting individually, especially when facing intractable problems following the energy crisis of 1973, inflation, recession, and massive unemployment.

Within the Communist bloc, the regional institutions were never more than pale counterparts of the Western institutions. The Soviet Union had separate bilateral arrangements with Communist China which broke down entirely by 1962. In Eastern Europe, they established the C.M.E.A. (Council for Mutual Economic Assistance; COMECON) as a counter to the Marshall Plan and the E.E.C., and the Warsaw Pact to meet the challenge of NATO. Both Organizations merely served to institutionalize

Soviet hegemony and did not prove really effective. From 1962 the Russians began to plan to endow C.M.E.A. with supranational powers in order to prevail against the persistent economic nationalism among its members and to slow down their individual attempts to improve their economic links with the West. This was not, however, successful and during the seventies a rapidly increasing proportion of the C.M.E.A. members' trade was diverted to the West.

The Warsaw Pact was mobilized only once, in August 1968, not for its avowed purpose of defence against NATO but to subdue and occupy one of its own members, Czechoslovakia, and to prevent her from developing an individual style—of a liberalized socialist regime unacceptable to the Russians. In contrast to the C.M.E.A., however, the Pact effectively organizes the military forces of the Communist bloc, ensuring a much greater unity of strategy and organization than that of the opposing NATO. Since the disbanding of the COMINFORM (Communist Information Bureau) in 1954, there is no permanent institution in charge of the ideological direction of Communist parties and states, but periodical international conferences of Communist parties take care of that. They oscillated between stressing Soviet leadership and 'polycentrism', the idea that the national paths to Communism may legitimately differ. In the early sixties they became a battlefield for the ideological struggle between the Soviet Union and China; in the seventies, when China absented herself from these conferences, new ideological struggles arose from the individual orientation of 'Euro-Communism', especially of the Italian Communist Party.

Further regional and subregional organizations came into being in the post-war period. Whereas their historical predecessor, the O.A.S. (Organization of American States) was not very effective in buttressing the United States' influence over the continent or in organizing and representing it in another fashion, the O.A.U. (Organization for African Unity) became an important international actor in representing the struggle against colonialism and racialism by the African states. Similarly, the Arab League became instrumental in co-ordinating the Arab anti-Israeli policies. All these organizations, however, could not fully control their members even on their main issue of interest; they were completely ineffective in the recurrent outbreaks of conflicts, sometimes very violent ones. Other regional organizations took longer to become established, e.g. ASEAN (Association of East Asian Nations), or were merely attempted.

Governments combine not only on a regional and/or ideological basis but also for specific functional purposes, whenever an activity transcends national boundaries, e.g. traditionally in the fields of international communications and in the control of international rivers. Although, on the whole, politically less important than the regional organizations so far discussed, the functional ones are much more numerous; they constitute the overwhelming majority of the intergovernmental organizations of which there were at least 280 in 1972. Some of them deal with technologies which are clearly of central importance, e.g. telecommunications, aviation, outer space, nuclear energy. Although for the convenience, sometimes approaching necessity, of smooth international co-operation these organizations tend to operate without much publicity, the complex politics underlying their operation occasionally breaks out.

Owing to the central importance of oil for the economies of the world, one of the best-known and politically most significant of these organizations is OPEC (Organization of Petroleum Exporting Countries). The Organization is sometimes referred to as a successful cartel of oil producers but this omits its important characteristic of being an organization of governments and not of oil companies. Admittedly its original and basic aims are concerned with oil as a commercial commodity, with the regulation of its flow and its pricing. Owing to a growing oil scarcity in the early seventies, OPEC made use of the new round of the Arab/Israeli wars to quadruple the price of oil; in the subsequent lingering world recession in which oil demand slumped, its solidarity was greatly weakened. OPEC, especially its Arab subsection, AOPEC, has also an explicitly political significance. The Arab oil producers used 'the oil weapon' in 1973 to exercise pressure against Israel and could conceivably do so again. Moreover, the Organization as a whole has the potential for developing a common policy towards a really substantial aid to the poorer countries and towards North/South issues in general.

All these intergovernmental organizations, both regional and functional are in essence extensions of nation-states which enable them to pursue their interests and to exercise influence. To some extent they infringe, of course, on the sovereignty of their members, especially when they become the instruments of the foreign policies of their leaders and most powerful participants. Universal international organizations, the United Nations and its Specialized Agencies, are more than that. They also are agencies which act on behalf of the international system as a whole, and therefore they will be more appropriately discussed in the latter context in Chapter 8. The United Nations and its collective security system do not, however, try to do away with the system of sovereign states. On the contrary, they can be considered as an attempt, admittedly not a particularly promising one, to perpetuate this system through a collective guarantee for all the member-states. Within the United Nations system, the individual states are still most powerful. They try desperately hard to preserve their own sovereign positions, although they are often much less careful regarding the sovereign positions of others. It is unnecessary for our purposes to identify all the voting blocs operating in the General Assembly and to discuss their performance. It suffices to mention the existence of these blocs and the fact that, on many issues, states no longer take an individual stand but are governed rather by bloc considerations.

The element that is least concrete, but nevertheless important in the United Nations, is that of an international community. Although inter-governmental in form and relying mainly on the support and actions of its member-states, the United Nations has occasionally been acting on behalf of this community. Since, however, the greater part of international relations still hinges around the actions of individual states, the machinery through which these states operate will have to be analysed first.

Interstate non-governmental actors

There is a basic physical reason for the dominance of states in international relations: they are in control of the whole habitable surface of the earth and, since any other organization must operate somewhere, it must either acquire the control of a state or become subject to one. Indeed, the history of mankind is full of examples of such mergers and often it is not quite clear whether the state or the other grouping is predominant. It is possible to consider Communism as an instrument of state policy of the Soviet Union, but it is also possible to consider the Soviet Union as an instrument of Communism; the Catholic Church may be subject to the state, but, again, the state may be subject to the Church. Without deciding on the merits of either interpretation, it is possible to agree that in many situations internationally important organizations and groupings tend to merge with states.

In the post-war period, however, the interdependence of the world has greatly increased and there have arisen numerous powerful cross-national (sometimes called transnational) actors and forces. State boundaries began to lose their traditional meaning as being of ultimate political importance; for some purposes, they became no more than discontinuities in the flow of transnational transactions, often obstructing the meeting of some human needs. The traditional state-centric view of the international system came under a sustained attack by a school of writers, a large part of which was based upon the identification of non-state actors and the analysis of their role.

Some of these have been in existence for a long time and among them churches are the oldest and best known, especially the Church of Rome, often referred to as the Vatican or the Holy See. Traditionally the Vatican has been treated as a sovereign state, although its present territory is scarcely 200 acres, and for a while it had no territory at all. The Vatican maintains diplomatic relations with well over forty states, not all of which are Christian, and also hierarchical relations with many hundreds of millions of Catholics scattered all over the world. By virtue of its spiritual supremacy over the faithful, the Vatican can exercise political influence over states in which these are a majority or a substantial minority. Needless to say, difficulties sometimes arise, especially in relations with Communist states in which Catholics are treated with great suspicion. The non-Catholic Christian Churches, organized since 1954 into the World Council of Churches, do not play an analogous political part, nor do the other great religions. Buddhism has never had a central organization, Islam possesses none since the abolition of the Caliphate in 1923, nor does Judaism, despite its new spiritual centre in Israel.

The new interstate non-governmental organizations rarely reach real political importance but have been extremely rapidly growing in numbers. Leaving apart Multinational Corporations (M.N.C.s) and terrorist and revolutionary groups, on which later, in 1972 *The Yearbook of International Organisations* listed as many as 2,190 such organizations against a mere 1,000 in 1958. Many of these organizations play the role of fairly independent actors in their individual fields of endeavour. It is likely, however, that the degree of their autonomy is directly related to the relative political unimportance of their field of activities—chess players or folk-lorists, for example, are bound to enjoy much greater independence from governmental interference than organizations active in the field of telecommunications.

The really important transnational elements are economic. At first the great trading organizations, like the English and the Dutch East India companies, started as purely commercial ventures. They could not, however, conduct their trade without a degree of political control over their sources of supply, and their activities became increasingly political and military. After they had reached sufficient importance, the state invariably stepped in. The financial interests of the eighteenth and nineteenth centuries are epitomized in the fabulous Rothschild family. Between 1811 and 1816 the five sons of Amschel Rothschild established themselves as important bankers in five European financial capitals. While maintaining close links among themselves, they became providers of finance for their respective governments and, despite severe competition, their near-monopoly remained unimpaired for some three generations.

Then there arose the great industrial empires and corporations. Their interests extended beyond state-boundaries and became intermingled with state-policies. In the nineteenth century they could and sometimes did ask their national governments to acquire territory which they needed for supplies of raw materials or as markets. It is, however, a fallacy to attribute all imperialism to this factor, as Marxists do. In fact on many, perhaps most, occasions, it was the reverse; the governments used economic interests in order to promote national expansion. The corporations had the alternative of straight competition with their foreign rivals, but this was hindered by governmental restrictions on free trade and often was not very profitable. The usual solution was found in co-operation through international cartels, but these again were sometimes used by states for political purposes. For instance, the cartel arrangements between German and American firms in the inter-war periods in chemical, light metal, and plastics industries, succeeded in preventing the production of strategically essential materials in the United States because they were more profitably obtained in Germany. Only when the Second World War broke out did the Americans realize to what extent their military potential had thus been weakened.

Giant M.N.C.s today maintain direct relations with foreign governments through their equivalents of foreign ministries and ambassadors. Especially prominent are the seven giant international oil companies, including Royal Dutch Shell and British Petroleum, Unilever, some chemical giants, Krupp, the companies representing American interests in copper in Chile, in sugar in the Dominican Republic, in fruit in the so-called 'banana republics'. In contrast to their predecessors in previous centuries, on the whole these corporations operate independently and do not seek government protection, except in the cases of nationalization of their foreign establishments which have become frequent since 1945. Government protection is not, indeed, of much avail, as is shown by the gradual nationalization of Western oil interests in the Middle East in the post-war period, despite the fact that they belonged to the most powerful corporations domiciled in the most powerful states, especially the United States. Sometimes governments intervene in the policies of the corporations, and, having the ultimate power, are obeyed. Thus American Administrations successfully restricted trade with Nazi Germany in 1940–1 and prevailed on the American oil companies to refrain from purchasing or carrying nationalized Persian oil in 1952. The industrial empires, however, are not fully subservient. Even in wartime some trade with enemy states continued and the trade restrictions directed against Communist countries and against Rhodesia were often avoided.

The question to what extent M.N.C.s' economic powers are encroaching upon the political sovereignty of states is controversial but need not be discussed and cannot be decided in the abstract. There exist no generally accepted criteria for classifying what constitutes an M.N.C. and individual authors disagree about these. Useful analytical categories developed about them include the concepts of the states involved in their activities, the home state and the host state; the degree and nature of the control exercised by the two; the basic type of enterprise (extractive, agricultural, manufacturing, service, financial, or conglomerate); the ownership of the subsidiaries; the degree of autonomy of the subsidiaries towards the parent firm which has been aptly classified into the ethnocentric, polycentric, and geocentric types.

The most prominent is, however, the economic dimension—the strength of the corporation. Sometimes this is very crudely measured by comparing the average sales of the giant corporations with the G.D.P.s (Gross Domestic Products) of states, revealing the staggering fact that in the early seventies eight giant corporations (General Motors, Ford, Standard Oil of New Jersey, Royal Dutch Shell, General Electric, Chrysler, Unilever, and Mobil Oil) were among the forty economically largest entities of the world; the leading giants had average sales some hundred times larger than the G.D.P.s of small poor new states. Different and somewhat more sophisticated indicators are found in an equally staggering figure of the added values accrued in the operations of these corporations.

As in the inconclusive debate about the power of states, these indicators of the economic strength of the corporations are meaningful not in absolute terms but only in their relative contexts. It is important to ascertain the political influence of the corporation both in the home and the host state—how central are its operations for the economy and how much political influence can it wield, what are the countervailing powers? We have on record the saying that 'what is good for General Motors is good for the United States' which, in a limited sense, is incontrovertible. In relations with host states relying upon one major item of exports, be it in mining or agriculture, the position of an M.N.C. yielding monopoly powers in the state's trade in this article is economically strong, but states have now become increasingly less helpless in their relationships through a combination of external forces favourable to them, especially the support of anti-capitalist states of the Third World organized for the purposes of such matters into the so-called Group of Seventy-seven, the existence of the General Assembly as a forum for complaints, and the sensitivity of public opinion in the home countries of the major multinationals.

For a while Marxists expected that the clarion call for the proletarians of all countries to unite would spell the end of national boundaries, but the First World War, in which the majority of the socialists in the various countries rallied behind their national governments, ended this illusion. The several successive Socialist Internationals did not have much impact on interstate relations. Their Communist successors were international only in form; the inter-war Comintern, which organized the Communist parties throughout the world, was under the Russian thumb and served as an instrument of Russian national policy; even more so was its more limited post-war successor, the COMINFORM, which was formally disbanded in 1954. Other political internationals such as the liberal one, or organizations of Eastern European Exiles, have no great political significance.

International trade union federations are another offspring of the Marxist idea of the international solidarity of workers, although, as is obvious in Britain and open avowed in the United States, trade unions have become fully nationalized and are mainly concerned with obtaining bigger slices of the respective national cakes. The two mammoth international organizations which have come into being since the war, the Communist-dominated World Federation of Trade Unions (W.F.T.U.) and the Western-dominated International Confederation of Free Trade Unions (I.C.F.T.U.) are engaged less in asserting internationally distinctive trade-unionist interests, than in supporting their respective sides in the cold war, particularly in competing for influence over the politically important trade unions in the new states.

Intranational actors

It is characteristic of the blurring of the traditional division lines between domestic and international politics that non-governmental groups and even individuals located primarily within a single state can attain the position of international actors. *Potentially* any issue of domestic politics can assume a sufficiently important international dimension to become conducive to a foreign policy objective, and hence any group or individual with a foreign policy objective can become such an international actor. This is a fairly new factor in international politics to which must be added the traditional factor that all interest groups of any importance are relevant to the stability and change in government and hence relevant, although only indirectly, to foreign policy. An explanation of how such domestic groups become international actors, i.e. fairly autonomous elements within international politics, is best provided by examples.

Take, for instance, a consumer protection group aiming at a far-reaching improvement in the safety standards of cars, like that of Ralph Nader, an individual who organized one in the United States. It would generally start operating as an orthodox domestic pressure group, trying to induce the government to introduce suitable domestic legislation to enforce the desired standards with the home producers and to exclude imports falling below them. Inevitably such domestic arrangements have international repercussions as the interests of the producers of the car imports are affected and, if the country is itself a car-exporter, also its external markets, as long as the foreign competitors in them would be free from keeping similar safety standards and hence enjoy lower production costs. All these international activities, although induced by the group, have been governmental and hence the group cannot be regarded as an international actor.

However, as happens in an increasing number of fields, the government may be unwilling or incapable of attaining the objectives of the consumer group which can logically lead it to seek the support of similar forces outside, especially among the major importers and exporters of cars; it would then help to organize similar groups in other states and link forces with those already in existence. This may finally lead to complete internationalization—the establishment of an international association of consumer protection groups which could operate quite autonomously. One can thus think of a spectrum of consumer protection groups according to their internationalization.

The problems are somewhat different with ethnic, racial, religious, or ideological minorities, the starting-point of which is found not in the international extension of their functional objectives but in their original link with a foreign country. The degree of their internationalization can again be regarded as constituting a spectrum. At the one end is activity as a traditional domestic pressure group trying to influence the policies of the home government in a direction favourable to the outside state with which they are linked. For instance, like other ethnic groups, the Jews in the United States have been generally operating as what is sometimes called 'the Zionist lobby', a pressure group aiming at making American foreign policy more favourable to the state of Israel. At times, however, the target changes and, especially in the late seventies, the 'Zionist lobby' was trying to induce the Israeli government to become more accommodating in negotiations with Egypt. Likewise, Western Communist parties which operate primarily as domestic political parties generally endeavour to influence the policies of their respective domestic governments in favour of the Soviet Union. In the late seventies, however, the Soviet Government also became their target; they came out in favour of greater respect for the protection of human rights, as provided by the Final Act of the Helsinki Conference of 1975. A similar analysis can be applied to human rights protection groups in their national and international activities.

Classifying the activities of a subnational group according to its target thus offers a convenient element for the analysis of their activities—according to whether they operate more on the home or on another government. It is, however, no yardstick for the classification of the groups themselves which, as the examples show, often aim at both targets. It seems best to abide by the criterion that an international actor must be a fairly autonomous agent in international politics and hence to consider groups whose target is limited to their home government as merely potential international actors.

There is, however, one type of subnational group which is of special importance even if its target is so limited—comprising those organized to remove the government. Such an organized group, when capable of replacing the government, be it through the electoral processes or force, is clearly significant as it may become the government; even if not fully successful, it may disturb governmental activities. The nomenclature of the groups relying on force is confused and confusing because it is extremely difficult to find an emotionally neutral name which would free it from ideological connotations. What is 'freedom' or 'independence fighters' or 'resistance movement' to the supporters of change becomes 'terrorists' to the supporters of the *status quo*. In a spirit of neutrality they will be called 'resistance movements' or 'fighters'. Again an example will serve best the purpose of elucidating the international role of such groups, especially the history of the Palestine resistance movement which in its evolution demonstrates the meaning and significance of the dimensions suggested and has been, moreover, the most important international actor in this category.

Widespread Arab opposition to the settlement of Jews in Palestine under an international mandate in the inter-war period was the background of a Palestinian resistance movement after the establishment of the state of Israel following a war in 1948 and the subsequent mass exodus of Arabs from Palestine. Although *unity* of purpose among the movement was ensured by their common goal—opposition to Israel—unity of organization remained an unattainable but constantly pursued goal. The physical dispersion of the refugees and the dependence of each group on one of Israel's close neighbours allied with the conflicts among the Arab states and their rulers, obstructed unity. The first of the major organizations, Al Fatah, which was formed in 1956–7, was largely dependent upon Syria whereas the Palestine Liberation Organization (P.L.O.) was established in Cairo to provide the Egyptians with a leverage. The 1967 'Six Days War' which ended in a crushing Arab defeat and in a new exodus of refugees invigorated the resistance movement, ensuring the strengthening of its political objective, a great supply of manpower and equipment while guerrilla successes in other parts of the world, especially Algeria and Vietnam, provided encouragement. At the same time, however, the proliferation of uncontrollable guerrilla groups made the forging of organizational unity even more difficult. Against the background of intrigues and manoeuvres the momentum towards unity reached its peak in 1968 in a formal reconciliation effected at a Palestinian National Assembly at Cairo. Soon however, the P.L.O. was faced by a military mutiny of some of its supporters and, in the following year, Fatah began to dominate it, having its leader, Arafat, elected as the chairman of the P.L.O. This ensured no unity, as even the united Organization could not exercise control over the more

radical elements of the movement and over the national com-
mando groups formed in the individual Arab countries. The latter
inevitably became the primary concern of each individual host
country, leading to violent conflicts and even civil wars, exemplified in the crushing of the Palestine resistance movement by
Jordan in 1971 and the Civil War in the Lebanon in 1976.

The resistance movement obtained a great degree of publicity,
largely as the result of spectacular terrorist activities in the sixties
and, despite all the intra-Arab conflicts which helped to deprive it
of unity, also a high degree of *legitimacy* in principle. A meeting of
the Arab League in Cairo in 1969 declared the P.L.O. to be
representative of the Palestine Arabs, blocking for some time the
possibility of local peace arrangements between Israel and her
neighbours, Jordan and Egypt. A degree of broader international
recognition followed—the G.A. invited Arafat to address its meeting and the Arab delegation to the abortive Geneva Peace Conference in 1973 included P.L.O. representatives. The P.L.O. became
a widely-recognized international actor. It was, however, subsequently outflanked by uncontrollable radical splinter movements
and thus weakened by continuing feuds among Arab states, giving
rise to a dramatic bilateral peace initiative between Egypt and
Israel in 1977–9.

As is the case with the conception of national interest in
sovereign states, the *objectives* and *strategies* of the P.L.O. were
changing following changes in circumstances. Starting with a
programme of the elimination of Israel and the return of the
Palestinian refugees to their original homes, the P.L.O. gradually
shifted to a demand of statehood for the Palestinian Arabs, merely
restricting Israel to her pre-1967 boundaries; its strategy gradually
shifted from terrorism to diplomacy and from seeking support
primarily in the Communist bloc to one seeking legitimacy in the
eyes of the other states. As the Israelis, however, understandably
argued, the change of emphasis towards much greater moderation
not only may have been merely a matter of convenient tactics but
was also vulnerable to a sudden change of leadership which could
be caused by the assassination of Arafat.

Finally, the *capabilities* of the Palestinian resistance movement
have been really substantial, including not only small arms but
even short-range rockets. The supply of equipment from Soviet

sources, whether directly or indirectly, and of money from rich Arab sympathizers, was ample. Moreover, the P.L.O. developed a broad international network with other radical fighter groups whose personnel occasionally participated in its para-military operations and who in turn were offered training facilities and equipment in P.L.O. centres.

In sum, although in its original form the Palestine resistance movement can be best regarded as a national subgroup with ramifications in neighbouring countries, in the seventies it became a very important regional and even global actor which played a much more significant role in international politics than many a sovereign state.

Finally, regarding the role of individuals in international politics, one must remember that international actors are defined by their relative autonomy. One source of confusion about the role of individuals in such a capacity, similar to one found in international law, is that individuals have traditionally been the objects and not the subjects of both; the growing concern with human rights since 1945 does not alter the situation. The second reason for confusion is that an individual often becomes an important international actor by virtue of the organizational role he plays. Naturally the personality of the incumbent of such prominent positions as the President of the United States or the Secretary-General of the United Nations is important; even more clearly so is the personality of a leader of a smaller state whose autonomy and influence may be entirely out of proportion to the relative unimportance of his state—Nasser of Egypt or Tito of Yugoslavia are striking examples. As it is difficult to unravel the amount of personal and institutional significance in such cases, it seems advisable to limit this category of international actors to individuals who are occasionally able to behave autonomously in their purely private capacity, although they could generally be expected to attract some organizational support. To choose among the diverse though few cases, one may mention the Norwegian explorer Fritjof Nansen, who originated international protection for refugees, the American Andrew Carnegie who endowed a peace research institution, the Swede Count Gustaf van Rosen who organized the rebel air force during the Nigerian Civil War, and the Argentinian revolutionary Ché Guevara. All these individuals acted in relatively limited fields and not many significantly active individuals could be added to this list. The ineffective attempts by the well-known British philosopher, Bertrand Russell, to act as an intermediary between the Russian and the American leaders of his day show how limited is the scope in the mainstream of international politics.

5 The making of foreign policy[1]

The process and the constitutional machinery

It is customary to personify states and to speak of 'British foreign policy' or 'British decisions', but in fact these are not made by the state but by single individuals and groups who act on its behalf. Theirs, like all other human activities, can be considered in terms of interaction between the decision-makers and their environment.

Most human needs and desires cannot be satisfied without some form of action, and this is generally preceded by a decision, meaning an act of will determining in one's mind the course of action to be taken. Decisions and resulting actions are the product of a confrontation in the minds of the decision-makers of their wants and desires with what they know about their environment. It is this psychological environment, the *image* of reality that people hold, which plays a part in their decisions, however much such an image may deviate from the environment as it really is.

The fundamentals are identical, but decisions taken on foreign policy differ from those taken in other fields in that they are subject to a unique interplay between domestic and foreign environments. The persons involved usually occupy certain official positions of trust and importance empowering them to act on behalf of their society in its external relations. It is the values of this society which they are to uphold; it is the interests of this society which they represent. When, however, they engage in their jobs, they are confronted by statesmen and officials belonging to other domestic societies and pursuing their own values and interests. Thus the international environment often proves intractable; statesmen sometimes face insuperable obstacles when pursuing the interests of their respective countries and they are constantly subject to pressures which are at variance with domestic pressures. The tradi-

[1] This chapter condenses part of the arguments in *The Making of Foreign Policy* (1963, 1967) and *National Interest* (1970) by the author.

tional image of foreign policy-making is that it consists of a rational assessment of the best means to attain certain established goals and objectives, overcoming the obstacles and using the opportunities offering in the external environment. Detailed analysis of some outstanding cases of decision-making, especially of crisis situations in the United States, have divulged that many aspects of the process are determined by its inner dynamics and by political rather than by rational processes. Especially since Professor Graham T. Allison has analysed the Cuban Missile Crisis of 1962 in these terms, many treatments have concentrated upon his alternative models: the 'organizational process' model which centres upon the interaction among loosely co-ordinated semi-independent groups within the government and the 'bureaucratic politics' model which centres upon the political manoeuvring of individuals. These somewhat overlapping models for studying the decision-making processes have been extremely popular in many subsequent analyses and can be regarded as an extremely useful complement to although by no means a substitute for the traditional 'rational' model.

Political life does not invariably conform to legal rules determining competence, but in the making of foreign policy the *formal* decision-makers are particularly important. Governments on the whole fully monopolize the control of foreign policy. This is partly due to the historical traditions dating from the absolutist period, and partly to the logic of the present situation, in which, as a rule, governments alone deal with other governments, command the best sources of information, and have the monopoly of legitimate, and a near-monopoly of physical, force. Any influence on foreign policy coming from other sources must be exercised through governments.

Although domestic political systems greatly vary from country to country and from period to period, certain uniformities do exist. The head of state does not usually play an effective part in foreign policy and his participation is mainly ceremonial. Exceptions can be found only in countries where the head of the state combines executive functions with his office—as the Presidents of the United States or of the Fifth French Republic. Powers are concentrated in the hands of the government, or, as the Americans call it, the executive, and within it, in the hands of its head and of the minister of foreign affairs (in Britain called the Secretary of State for Foreign Affairs or Foreign Secretary for short, in the United States called the Secretary of State). Other elements which should be taken into account are legislatures; the civil servants in the foreign ministry and in certain other, for the purposes of foreign policy, subsidiary departments; and public opinion. All these will be considered in turn.

The head of the government and his foreign minister

The head of the government usually plays a decisive role. In the presidential system in the United States the members of his cabinet are merely his advisers and, although this is somewhat over-simplified, it is fundamentally true, as President Truman remarked, that 'the President makes foreign policy'. In Britain major policy decisions are generally taken by the Cabinet as a whole, but the Prime Minister is fairly free in the choice of its members and leads its deliberations. Moreover, we have on record several important instances when the Prime Minister did not consult the Cabinet as a whole on major foreign policy moves; the Suez expedition in 1956 is a case in point. He is normally sure of the loyalty of his Cabinet colleagues and of the support of his party members in parliament; provided his parliamentary majority is reasonable, his power is secure. This is not so with coalition governments, such as that headed by Winston Churchill during the last War.

The head of the government generally chooses a foreign minister to his liking but he may be restricted by party priorities or coalition requirements. The minister is subordinate, but, when the head of the government lacks any special interest in foreign policy and fully trusts him his may be the decisive voice. To some extent this was quite recently the case with Ernest Bevin in the Attlee Governments in Britain and with John Foster Dulles in the Eisenhower Administrations in the United States. The modern tendency, however, is for the heads of government to assume personal responsibility for major foreign policy decisions; very occasionally they combine the two offices despite the crippling amount of work involved. In any case, they are personally involved in the increasingly more frequent 'summit meetings' which have been made possible by modern communications.

Even when personally conducting foreign policy, the head of the government cannot help leaving large areas of activity to his minister. When the views of the two are closely related, no serious problems of co-ordination arise, but where they diverge, in time the head would tend to remove the minister from office or by-pass him by using other ministers or personal agents.

In the Soviet Union and in other Communist states, real power is vested in the Communist parties rather than in the traditional governmental machineries which they all possess, though it is possible to exaggerate the unimportance of the latter. Undoubtedly the First Secretary of the Communist Party is the key figure, even if he does not combine his office with that of the President of the Council of Ministers, as, for a while, both Stalin and Khrushchev did. While Stalin was omnipotent within the Party, his successors have to tolerate opponents and depend on decisions taken by their colleagues, admittedly those in the Politburo rather than in the Council of Ministers. Their position differs in degree rather than in kind from that of the heads of government elsewhere.

The developing states are governed by a variety of governments which fall into a wide spectrum; at the one extreme are those completely autocratic, with the head of the government often being a military figure; at the other, those which are democratic in the sense that the government can be removed through the electoral process. In all cases, however, there is a strong tendency for a much greater concentration of power in the hands of the top-leader and for a much less articulated political system below them than we find in older countries.

Legislatures

Discussion here must be limited mainly to the Western democracies since, with the partial exception of India, parliamentary institutions, when they exist elsewhere, do not wield real powers.

Parliamentary powers are generally smaller in foreign than in domestic affairs, but even so they can be important. They vary from country to country and they are determined by an interplay between fairly stable constitutional arrangements and such more ephemeral elements as the political climate, the strength of the parties, and the characters of the leading personalities. One extreme can be found in the United States, where the principle of 'checks and balances' and the absence of party discipline ensure the Congress a role co-ordinate with that of the executive; the other in the Soviet Union, where the Supreme Soviet lacks any effective powers; other systems lie somewhere in between.

Being large and clumsy bodies, parliaments cannot effectively initiate foreign policy and are limited to the exercise of the power of veto over policies proposed by governments. Their main legal power usually lies in the ratification of treaties. In a particularly stiff form, the American Constitution requires the concurrence of a two-thirds majority of the Senate. This led to repeated rejections of treaties which culminated in the refusal to ratify the Peace Treaty of Versailles in 1919 but, since then, improved methods of consultation, bi-partisanship, and the employment of 'Executive Agreements' which do not require ratification have rendered the Senate's powers much less formidable. Also in a multi-party system refusal of ratification can have serious effects; for example, in the Fourth French Republic parliament threw out the European Defence Community Treaty in August 1954. The British House of Commons lacks legal powers of ratification, although it has the opportunity to debate important treaties which, under the convention of the so-called 'Ponsonby Rule', lie on the table for three weeks before their ratification by the government.

All legislatures which exercise real power hold the purse-strings and governments depend upon them to allocate the funds required for foreign policy. This is a telling power today when defence expenditure usually constitutes one of the main items of the budget and foreign aid is widely given. It is one of the major reasons why the House of Representatives is becoming increasingly important in the making of American foreign policy. Parliaments are also required to pass any laws which may be necessary to implement international treaties.

Legislatures can go beyond that and continuously control foreign policy through their standing committees. This has happened particularly in the United States where such committees employ staff independent of the Executive, are constantly consulted by the State Department, and conduct investigations and hearings. The Chairman of the Senate Committee on Foreign Relations occupies a key position which, at times, may be more important than that of the Secretary of State. The House of Commons has not established a standing committee on foreign affairs, in order to avoid the inevitable consequence of sometimes embarrassing the Foreign Office and of depriving it of much of its flexibility. It exercises only intermittent control through extensive foreign policy debates and also through questions put to the Government at Question Time.

Civil service

An important distinction is usually drawn between policy-making and administration. In theory, the ministers make the policy while the officials merely execute it but it is scarcely possible to exaggerate the importance of the bureaucratic machinery. Its members preserve the continuity of policy, while foreign ministers of different parties and views come and go. Moreover, these ministers—and also heads of governments—usually rise to power on the basis of their achievements in the field of domestic politics; when they assume their responsibilities for foreign affairs, they naturally become dependent on expert advice.

It is difficult and somewhat futile to decide to what extent a minister makes decisions or merely confirms decisions made by his officials. This is only of academic interest when they do not differ in their views; when they do, the politicians generally prevail, though only in the long run. In Fascist Italy and in Nazi Germany the permanent officials who rejected or only half-heartedly accepted the policies of their masters were by-passed and eventually removed; in Britain, when Neville Chamberlain clashed with the Foreign Office over his policy of appeasement, he removed Lord Vansittart from his powerful position of Permanent Under-Secretary and continuously by-passed diplomatic channels, using for the purpose his personal agent, Sir Horace Wilson.

Nevertheless, where policies are less firm and clashes less pronounced, the advice of the officials carries much weight, and, if it is ignored, the implementation of policies contrary to their views may be slowed down or even actively obstructed. The ingrained attitudes of the permanent officials should be neither minimized nor exaggerated. On the one hand, it is unlikely that a British Foreign Secretary would succeed with a pronouncedly pro-Israel policy against the pro-Arab traditions of the Middle Eastern

Department; the Foreign Office traditions of giving only lukewarm support to international organization and, until the late fifties, of lack of sympathy with European integration, may have strongly contributed to British policies in these fields. On the other hand, the French Foreign Ministry must have gone through a fundamental reappraisal before embarking on the policy of integration with Germany. Bureaucracy is particularly prominent in France where it provides the main element of continuity in the constant change of constitutions and governments. In the Federal Republic of Germany, it has survived the War as one of the least affected centres of power and has been confirmed in its traditional importance by the occupation authorities, but apparently the average German official remains indifferent to politics beyond his narrow specialist domain.

Little information is available about the secretive working of Soviet bureaucracy. In terms of power, the Soviet equivalent of Western foreign ministries is probably the Foreign Department of the Central Committee of the Communist Party, the various sections of which maintain close relations with the corresponding sections of the Foreign Ministry. Stalin's personal secretariat—the so-called 'technical cabinet'—an institution perpetuated by Khrushchev and his successors, probably still continues to play a central part in Soviet domestic politics and, in all likelihood, influences also the determination of foreign policies.

The enormous increase in the scope of international relations has led to the blurring of the traditional demarcation lines between domestic and foreign affairs in governmental machineries. Despite the fact that foreign ministries are now grossly overworked, most other departments are involved in many foreign issues, giving rise to grave problems of co-ordination. The situation is most acute in the United States owing to its transition from the restrictions of isolationism to the expansion of world leadership. In 1949 no less than forty-five out of the identified fifty-nine departments, commissions, boards, and inter-departmental councils were involved in some aspects of foreign affairs. In Britain eight ministries were seriously and continuously concerned in the negotiations with the European Economic Community between 1956 and 1958; presumably all these departments were involved also in the negotiations in 1961–3 and 1966–7; especially the Ministries of Trade and of Agriculture and Fisheries were constantly involved in Community negotiations. While co-ordination in Britain is undertaken through informal contacts and through Cabinet Committees, in the United States it has led to a confusing proliferation of bodies and to the employment of various methods, none of which has been really successful.

Soviet experience is characteristic of the problems involved. Until recently Soviet foreign policy, which is rigidly controlled by the Party, was much better co-ordinated than are foreign policies in the West. Since the last War, however, the Soviet Union has intensified and ramified its foreign relations—there are intimate links with other Communist governments as well as parties, foreign aid, delicate relations with the new, uncommitted countries, increased cultural and commercial exchanges with the West. Despite strict central control, difficulties of co-ordination at middle and lower levels are likely to arise. Most difficult of all, however, is the co-ordination of the frequently conflicting requirements of domestic and foreign policies, as exemplified in the continuing suppression of Soviet citizens concerned with the monitoring of human rights enshrined in the Final Act of the 1975 Helsinki Conference. Although the Soviet rulers suffered a great degree of opprobrium abroad to the detriment of their foreign policy, they apparently considered their policy necessary in order to keep domestic politics under control.

The administration of foreign affairs is partly decentralized since states maintain diplomatic missions in the capitals of all other states with which they have relations of any intensity or importance. Before the development of modern communications, diplomats in charge of missions could not receive prompt instructions from their ministries and were often forced to make major decisions on their own responsibility. Today this is rarely necessary, but foreign envoys are much more than mere subordinates following instructions. Not only do they supply and interpret information from the country of their sojourn but they can still be called upon to make a prompt decision on the spot if faced with a sudden minor emergency.

Subsidiary services

Foreign policy is not conducted by diplomacy alone; it relies heavily on the military forces and on the scientists who supply them with up-to-date weapons, on economists, and also, especially today, on intelligence and propaganda services. Absolutist rulers of the past could personally deal with all these matters, but now such integration is unthinkable and extensive specialized services have been developed. These services are generally merely subsidiary to diplomacy but in some circumstances they can exercise great influence upon the decision-making process—the military when it comes to securing strategic frontiers, or allies or bases; the scientists concerning the development of weapons; the intelligence services when they act without full governmental control or diplomatic guidance.

Of these, the military are by far the most important, although civilian control is the rule both in the West and in Communist countries where military dictatorships tend to represent themselves as mere stepping-stones towards civilian government. Of all the industrialized countries, it was only in Germany and Japan that the military had developed fairly independently of civilian control, but in neither have they recovered their independence since the Second World War.

Naturally, strategic and diplomatic considerations do sometimes clash, especially in wartime, but although the civilians can ignore military advice only at their peril and hence do not reject it lightly, they do so when it seems to them expedient. Matters are further complicated today by the policy of deterrence, in which the weapons are not supposed to be *used*, but only to *deter*. Hence success depends on *what* weapons are available, and this is in the hands of the scientists, and not only on *how* they are to be used, which is the traditional subject-matter of military strategy. Ever since 1937, after the potentialities of nuclear energy had been finally ascertained, some nuclear scientists did, indeed, try, though unavailingly, to interfere in politics to prevent the use of bombs against Japan and to bring them under international control. Their advice on new weapons and on the likely achievements of the rival Power, advice inevitably coloured by their political views, undoubtedly affects policy decisions.

Aid-administering agencies play a minor part in countries offering foreign aid, particularly in the United States, where they have been partly but never fully subordinated to the Department of

State. Similarly subordinate are the propaganda services, despite the great sums of money lavished upon them by all major Powers. More independent are the intelligence services, which tend to engage in cloak-and-dagger activities and pursue them beyond the mere collecting of information. The United States Central Intelligence Agency (C.I.A.) was conducting a foreign policy of its own for a number of years. It was responsible for the support of Chinese nationalists in Northern Burma, the U-2 reconnaissance flights over Soviet territory, the invasion of Cuba in 1961, and the opposition to left-wing governments in Latin America. Repeated presidential efforts to bring the C.I.A. under effective central control were necessary before the Agency was apparently curbed by the late seventies. It is difficult to identify the impact of the highly-diversified Soviet intelligence services but undoubtedly these, as well as the services of other major Powers, operating as they do in secret and with substantial funds, have ample opportunities for at least an occasional independent action.

Public opinion

It is unnecessary to postulate a democratic ideology or a theory of the 'general will' in order to acknowledge the ultimate importance of the people as a whole. As David Hume noted, 'It is . . . on opinion only that government is founded; and this maxim extends to the most despotic and most military governments as well as to the most free and most popular'. Public opinion comes to bear as an unorganized whole, in the form of a 'mood', which prescribes the limits within which policy can be shaped, and also through organized sectional interests and their leaders and intermediaries. Until 1914 public opinion was only marginally interested in foreign policy but, during the later stages of the First World War, the rapidly growing labour force began to insist on its popular control, as a key to a liberal peace. The new force was vulnerable to outside influence and was appealed to both by Wilson and by the Bolsheviks; the internationalists regarded it as the great weapon which would ensure peace.

This new element in the conduct of foreign policy has given rise to a host of problems most of which still remain unsolved. The people are generally poorly informed and, even if information is available to them, their judgement is often wrong. Here opinions vary—radicals tend to attribute some wisdom to the man in the street, while thinkers less radically inclined, especially practising diplomats, generally deprecate his powers of understanding. While the former favour more information for the public, the latter are inclined to withhold it on dangerous matters and to manipulate it in the direction desired. This ties up with the problems of guidance. The idea of democracy does not imply that the leaders should rigidly follow public opinion, but it does imply and sometimes even demands, that they should direct it.

It is not always easy to know the reaction of public opinion to any given issue. This is so even in Western democracies where the people's views are generally fairly articulate and are frequently ascertained in free elections and through public opinion polls. On an issue as important as that of Britain joining the Common Market, at the crucial moment in August 1961, when the government decided to apply for membership, the state of public opinion simply could not be guessed; the various sectional interests had not yet adopted a firm stand and the general public was completely ignorant of what was involved. Opinion became fully clarified as being favourable only during the second application in 1967, probably largely as the result of careful official manipulation.

In countries where political life has achieved a certain degree of sophistication, public opinion is structured and organized in political parties and pressure groups. Only a small proportion of the citizens may be interested, informed, and active in foreign policy matters, but those who are assume positions of leadership at various levels. Their opinions are indicative of the way in which public opinion is likely to react and they are the most promising people upon whom influence can be brought to bear. They are more influential than the popular press and other mass media, important as these are, in influencing public opinion.

In the rigidly governed Communist countries public opinion is not structured from below, as in the West, but organized from above, through a hierarchy of leadership. Here the extensive agitation-propaganda apparatus used for the purposes of discovering and manipulating public opinion has apparently been only partially successful.

In the well-integrated British and Western European societies, emotional appeals by a Mosley or a Poujade find little hearing, but in the somewhat less-integrated United States, Senator Joseph McCarthy was for a while a dangerous demagogical leader. In the many societies where political structures are rudimentary, the illiterate masses of unskilled and often unemployed urban workers are unstable in their recent divorce from their rural origins and unhappy in their wretched living conditions, while the students are aware of the shortcomings of their societies but are incapable of providing a rational or practical answer to their problems. Here radical nationalists and Communists have great scope for demagogic appeals.

National interest and national values

'National interest' is the key concept in foreign policy. In essence, it amounts to the sum total of all the national values—national in both meanings of the word, both pertaining to the nation and to the state. Inevitably this concept is rather vague. One common-sense definition describes it as the general and continuing ends for which the nation acts. It is thus characterized by its non-specific nature, by a degree of continuity, and by its connection with political action. A major ambiguity arises from the use of the concepts in different contexts without sufficient clarification. National interest can describe the *aspirations* of the state; it can be used also *operationally*, in application to the actual policies and programmes pursued; it can be used *polemically* in political argument, to explain, rationalize, or criticize. The recurrent controversies on foreign policy often stem from these ambiguities and not only from the different ideas about the substance of the national interest.

National interest need not be so narrowly defined as to exclude moral, religious, and other altruistic considerations, but, to be effective, these must have been accepted as part of it. In actual practice it may not always make much difference whether a decision is made by a statesman who subscribes to the Hegelian theory that the state is the supreme good (which is the foundation of totalitarianism) or by another who believes that the state is merely an instrument to satisfy the needs of the citizens. As long as the state remains responsible for the welfare of its citizens in most avenues of life and the purveyor of many social needs, both may interpret national interest in a similar way. They may, however, greatly disagree in the future as increasingly more human needs have to be satisfied outside the confines of the state. A narrow interpretation of national interest, based upon the idea that the state and its sovereignty must be preserved at all costs, would indicate a different general attitude to international management than a liberal one based upon the idea that only such organization is capable of meeting some important needs.

All statesmen are governed by their respective national interests, but this does not mean that they can never agree on anything. On the contrary, they often do, but only on the basis of their conceptions of these national interests. If a statesman agrees to concessions, he does so only when he is convinced that this brings some advantage to his state, directly or indirectly. For instance, the favourable treatment of the trade of another country may secure not only trade-openings but also friendship; support for a partly obnoxious international institution may be worthwhile in order to secure the continuation of its otherwise useful activities or to ensure international goodwill. Co-operation is conditional upon the existence of a suitable framework, of a reasonably stable international order within which the actions of other states are predictable and therefore rational foreign policy is possible. From here stems the interest of all states in this international order, again according to their individual national advantage. If they find this order congenial, they support it and, if necessary, defend it; if uncongenial, they endeavour to alter it accordingly.

At least for the time being, no alternative to one's own national interest is conceivable. If a statesman were to give his allegiance to the national interest of another country, this would be treason, and is extremely rare at the very top level of authority. If his first loyalty were to international organization rather than to his own state, he would be unlikely to rise to a position in which foreign policy decisions are made. On a liberal interpretation of national interest, clashes between national and international loyalties can usually be avoided, but if one does occur, the statesman's first duty is to his state.

The notion of 'national interest' is based upon the values of the national community, values which can be regarded as the product of its culture and as the expression of its sense of cohesion, values which define for men what they believe to be right or just. The relationship between these values and concrete policy objectives requires some explanation.

Values belong to the realm of the 'ought' and may or may not be translated into concrete political objectives. To say that the rulers of the Soviet Union are adherents of the Communist ideology means that they believe that Communism ought to prevail throughout the world, but not necessarily that they are actually pursuing concrete objectives to achieve it. The historical fact that Communism has been expansive throughout its existence indicates that the rulers actually do pursue such objectives, but a person wishing to analyse Soviet foreign policy should examine the question of whether concrete objectives remain intact after such events as Stalin's death. To say simply that, because Communist ideology makes the spread of Communism desirable, therefore the Communist leaders automatically pursue appropriate expansionist goals, may debar us from noticing a possible change in these goals. With equal profit, the Communists could abandon their confusion between the United States' desire to get rid of Communism (which is, indeed, an important element in Western ideology) and the aggressive strategic objectives which they impute to the Americans, to achieve this in practice.

Usually value-systems are loose and they often include conflicting values; on any concrete issue the problem arises how to find out which values apply. A case in point is trade with Communist China in the sixties. The British thought of it mainly in terms of achieving the maximum trade possible while the Americans were more concerned with the danger of strengthening a potential enemy; the issue was predominantly economic for the former but predominantly political for the latter. To make things worse, statesmen may be deliberately misleading in what they say; according to Freud, they may themselves be ignorant of their true motivations. Finally, different cultures do not attribute the same importance to the same values; there is, for instance, little meeting-ground between a Westerner who stresses economic values and a non-European who refuses to do so.

Throughout the history of political thought man has been seeking a supreme value which could be used as a general yardstick. Unfortunately the very fact that so many conflicting theories have arisen casts some doubt on the general validity of any one of them.

The popular yardstick of 'national interest' is too vague and that of 'power' is insufficient. Power has, in fact, been the necessary condition of self-preservation, and a state which ignores this condition persistently cannot escape the danger of disappearing. This does not mean that the yardstick is or can be persistently applied to all values in all situations; indeed, it is sometimes ignored and even deliberately acted against.

Whenever two or more values clash, the relative importance of both must be weighed and established, even if there can be no agreement on the identity of a supreme value. This 'ranking' of values is not easy because intensity fluctuates from case to case and is often determined by emotions. For example, a violation of national frontiers by a small detachment of an unfriendly neighbouring state may be considered as an unpleasant but purely local incident or it may be blown-up to a symbolic issue warranting retaliation, even to the lengths of waging war. In short, it is quite impossible to develop a rational 'value calculus' and choices among values are bound to remain largely intuitive.

Values in their interaction with the environment

Values reach their full political significance only in action, when the statesman actively applies them. In the vaguest and most general form this leads to what may be described as a vision of the good life, an arrangement of the elements of reality—as perceived by the decision-maker—to approximate as closely as possible to the values he holds. Needless to say when it comes to actual action, the vision can never be fully realized because the environment is always, at least to some degree, intractable. There is always some tension between the vision of the good life and life itself, even when the vision is so moderate that it can be easily translated into a concrete political programme. Some visions are quite Utopian, completely unrealizable, and most of them contain a sizeable Utopian element.

While the vision of the good life indicates only the general direction desirable for foreign policy, more specific principles of behaviour are deduced from it and, most importantly, also concrete political objectives—or ends or goals—which the statesman decide to pursue. The decision of how far they are prepared to go in their efforts to secure the values may be called the pitching of the level of aspirations. This level differs with the personality of the individuals and with national character which can be either predominantly optimistic, determined, ready to take risks, or predominantly pessimistic, cautious, preferring to play safe. It fluctuates also according to how successful action proves to be.

To arrive at a political decision, a statesman must juxtapose his values and his environment and therefore we must investigate how he arrives at his knowledge of this environment. The major link here is information, and, indeed, all foreign ministries and, within their specialized fields, also military authorities, assiduously collect it. However abundant, the open and legitimate sources of information are generally deficient in the most important matters and have therefore been traditionally supplemented by espionage.

Although top-level statesmen have full access to the information available to their governments, they cannot possibly digest it all. By the time information reaches them it tends to have become condensed and separated from reality to the point of allowing complete misinterpretation. This being so, skilful politicians can and often successfully do use their intuition. Personalities differ immensely in this respect. In recent American history we may contrast President Eisenhower, who refused to become acquainted with facts directly and relied on John Foster Dulles to bring to his attention anything of real importance, with the voracious appetite for information and the extraordinary range of Presidents Franklin D. Roosevelt and John F. Kennedy.

In order to select what is relevant from the bewildering variety of facts and events, one must have some criteria of relevance. Every country develops interpretative rules in accordance with its national culture and traditions, but generally these rules are not articulated and hence it is difficult to identify them and to change them if necessary. It is difficult to understand the rules of one's own country but, even more so, those employed by other national communities. Sometimes insufficient allowance is made for differences, for instance when the Appeasers regarded Hitler as a politician of the same school as themselves, who would rationally accept a chance of satisfying his avowed and fairly legitimate ambitions, or when the Czechoslovak leaders were confronted with the cynicism of their Russian counterparts during their enforced negotiations in Moscow in August 1968. It is equally dangerous to proceed on the assumption that the rules which govern the behaviour of others are completely different from one's own, a belief held strongly by some anti-Communists.

Interpretation is not fully rational but is often governed by emotions, by the tendency in people to develop 'blind spots' for what is unpleasant, and by wishful thinking. Also the underlying rational processes are unreliable. We can no longer accept the notion of causality as a fully adequate link among events; Communist dialectical processes of reasoning lead to interpretations vastly different from those based on Western formal logic; the Chinese or the Africans may find both unacceptable.

What we find out about our environment is thus so remote from reality that instead of speaking about 'knowledge' we should employ rather the word 'perception' or 'image'. The important feature of an image is its emphasis on the general outline rather than on detailed items of information. Once a statesman has formed an image of an issue or of another state, this image acts as an organizing device for further information and as a filter through which this information must pass. Images, not detailed information, govern political behaviour. Voters tend to be swayed by the image of the party rather than by specific electoral issues; statesmen deal with another state on the basis of their image of this state rather than on the merits of the concrete problem on hand. The ingrained respective images of a hostile Superpower governed the mutual relations of the Americans and the Russians much more than the details of their actual behaviour. Where this behaviour does not correspond with the image, it is simply ignored—the Russians took no notice of the elementary fact that the allegedly aggressive Americans did not destroy them when they had the monopoly of nuclear weapons, nor did the Americans acknowledge the conciliatory nature of some Soviet moves after Stalin's death.

One of the most significant relationships within the environment is the interaction between domestic and foreign affairs. On the basis of relative security and isolation from foreign affairs, it has been customary for British and American thinkers and statesmen to believe that the two domains are separable and that domestic affairs prevail. Very different is the tradition of the continental countries where such separation has never taken place. Even in powerful states like Napoleonic France or Bismarckian Germany, military requirements and foreign policy objectives invariably mingled with the basic issues of domestic politics. Small and weak states were always even more open to foreign influences. Hence the continental doctrine of necessity or *raison d'État*. Today, even in the West there is no agreement about the interrelations between domestic and foreign affairs—some think that all that states can do is to react to the imperious dictates of foreign policy, especially the implications of the nuclear dilemma; others have retained the idea that statesmen have a freedom of choice, although within environmentally prescribed limits.

Human minds and energy being limited, excessive concentration on either domestic or foreign affairs must be at the expense of one or the other. Thus during the isolationist era the United States grossly neglected its foreign affairs. Perhaps exaggeratedly, George Orwell described in *Nineteen Eighty-Four* the suppression of the individual in a 'garrison state' concerned only with its own survival. When popular discontent at home reaches an acute stage, governments often resort to the expedient of diverting attention from domestic to foreign affairs.

Often the domestic/foreign interrelation is blurred. Undoubtedly there was a close connection between Soviet policy in China in the later twenties and the dramatic struggle between Stalin and Trotsky at home, or between Soviet action in Hungary in 1956 and the relations between Khrushchev and his opponents. Nevertheless, it is an over-simplification to contend, as is sometimes done, that in both cases domestic considerations fully determined foreign policy, since in both cases the foreign reverses had, in turn, a profound effect on domestic policies. They rendered insecure the incumbents of office and impelled them to stress domestic change in order to divert attention from their failures abroad.

Particularly difficult are the problems of newly-established states where political life at home is generally unsettled and domestic pressures are often insuperable. Violent nationalism, which has brought these states into existence, dictates anti-imperialist and hence generally anti-Western policies, a situation which the Communists endeavour to exploit but which is unpalatable to many of the more responsible statesmen.

6 Interaction among states and state power

Core values and vital interests

So far states have been discussed singly, preparing the ground for the analysis of their interaction which constitutes the bulk of international relations. Here, the level of analysis employed must be constantly borne in mind: at the macropolitical level (discussed later in Chapters 7–10), this interaction is considered primarily as a function of the coexistence of the states in an historically established international system. First, however, we shall consider their interaction at the micropolitical level, looking at states from their individual perspectives as interacting in order to pursue certain interests and to meet certain contingencies arising in the international environment.

Before tackling the issue of how states interact, it is important to investigate what they are doing it for. Among the amorphous category of values and interests, states regard some as most important, often referring to them as 'vital interests'; scholars tend to use also the somewhat overlapping category of 'core values'. Decision-makers violently disagree on ultimate, supreme values as much as do philosophers: some seek them primarily in the individuals served by the collectivity of the state and others primarily in the collective which is to be served by its members; some pursue narrow nationalistic and others broad ecumenical values, be they ideological, religious, racial, or regional. Whatever the substance of their beliefs, they are all concerned above all with the preservation of the essential features of the social organization of their respective states. Three preliminary observations must be made about these. First, the primary values of the states are thus domestic and are pursued in the domestic sphere. This should be kept in mind when considering international relations since adjustments of domestic interests are constantly taking place and are complementary to international relations, and sometimes a full alternative to them. Second, the perceptions of the international environment held by the decision-makers are so crucial an element in their activities that academic conceptualizations remote from their ways of thinking should never be imputed to them or perhaps even employed in the early stages of the analysis, although they can be extremely useful for precise analytical or for normative purposes. A third point relates to our uncertainty about the basic nature of state interactions—are they mainly purposeful, rational acts, arising from the pursuit of certain objectives, or are they mere random actions and reactions arising from the historical configurations of the international and domestic systems? It is easy to agree that state interactions include an element of both but extremely hard to define how much of each category, especially in a concrete case.

Important as it is to state this question, it is possible to leave it open and to proceed with the analysis of the substance of the interactions—the meeting and clashes of interests among states. The clashes are particularly significant whenever they arise over vital interests, core values, so defined because people are attached to them to the point of being prepared to pay a very high cost for them, even of making ultimate sacrifices, and are not prepared to compromise. Traditionally the territorial integrity and political independence of a state have been regarded as such core values, at least in the last two centuries or so. In fact, however, as has been argued in Chapter 4, for some time we have been facing a crisis of the territorial state so that the traditional core values cannot be regarded as absolute because sovereignty is now never complete, and boundaries are always to some extent penetrated. It is merely a matter of degree to which these encroachments and penetrations are tolerable. Therefore the stark model of states confronting one another with conflicting and unmovable core values, however convincingly it seems to represent the situations leading to the two World Wars, does not seem to be appropriate to the situation towards the end of the twentieth century, at least until and unless really violent conflicts break out. Core values are not absolute and rigid and hence it is necessary to think of the categories useful for exploring their interpretation and transformation.

If we seek a modern redefinition of the traditional basic core values, we must first reduce them to what appears to be their common denominator, namely self-preservation. To repeat the point, in modern conditions such 'self-preservation' is defined no longer by the rigid adherence to the absolute concepts of territorial integrity and political independence, which have been eroded, but rather by more flexibly defined features, not only of the political but also of the socio-economic structure, making full allowance for ideological and cultural elements. In discussing the way in which states proceed, it is useful to apply the distinction made by the late Professor Arnold Wolfers between 'possession goals' based upon the preservation of absolute control by the state, like sovereignty over territory or powers to conduct autonomously one's external relations, and 'milieu goals' concerned with the shaping of the conditions in the international environment. If, as all the major advanced industrialized governments claim, it is a core value for each to preserve a national steel industry in the face of the threats to its continued existence by lower-costs rivals in newly developing states, the clash of interests with the vital interests of the rivals can be met by an adjustment in the evaluation of the interest, an acceptance that effective competition is impossible and consolation with the resulting cheaper price of steel. An alternative is the preservation of domestic industry by the exercise of state sovereignty through raising of tariff barriers—a policy now curbed by international agreements circumscribing this right. Another alternative is the elevation of the conflict to the category of milieu goals through arrangements made internationally, an expedient actually employed in the E.E.C. in the late seventies.

Role, self-sufficiency, and interdependence

One important factor among those determining the international behaviour of a state is found in its position and function within the international system, often referred to as the 'role'. This concept which is widely used and well-defined in sociology is much more diffuse in international relations; partly but not fully it coincides with the nineteenth-century concept of 'status', an important element in the ranking of states. By definition, the exact content of the 'role' is ambiguous: first, owing to the multi-functional nature of states which allows us to use a wide variety of possible yardsticks, and second because the definition of the role by the state's own decision-makers cannot be expected to coincide fully with role definitions by other states. Although no satisfactory and generally acceptable definition of 'role' has been produced, most thinkers distinguish three major dimensions of state behaviour which cannot, however, be readily accommodated into a meaningful general scheme: a spectrum between satisfied and dissatisfied, active and passive, powerful and weak states.

The major distinction frequently noted is between the state's own role definition and definitions made by others. It is notorious that policies regarded as 'defensive' by the actor are the very reverse—'aggressive' or 'offensive'—to others. This is demonstrated by the continuous mutual accusations of the Americans and the Russians, when they support various friendly regimes and establish alliances and bases abroad or engage in new weapons systems; the mutually conflicting role definitions of both differ from those produced by the Chinese. All these varying definitions refer, however, to the same phenomenon—the behaviour of states which is only variously interpreted, according to different yardsticks and priorities. This situation closely resembles differences in the perceptions of any other element of reality and requires the same kind of comparison not only of the various interpretations but also of their relationship to this reality.

A major underlying though poorly articulated and understood factor in international behaviour is the degree of self-sufficiency or dependence upon others. This concept has been somewhat blurred in the second part of the twentieth century owing to the rapid growth of what is often called 'interdependence', (on which later). By interdependence is meant a dependence upon the international system which is now common to all states as a condition of their existence, especially for their survival through preventing a major war and through preserving the minimum necessary of international trade and other exchanges. The situation used to be clearer in the past: a state with a large territory and ample natural resources could be regarded as capable of much more self-sufficiency than less well-endowed states. After 1945, for instance, only the two Superpowers seemed to have the conditions for a fair degree of self-sufficiency; China and the few small states trying to achieve it did so only at the cost of appallingly low living standards. Throughout the seventies, even the Superpowers were losing their self-sufficiency; the United States was becoming increasingly dependent on oil imports and the Soviet Union upon the imports of

Western technology. Both could reverse the trends and could survive the cutting off of supplies, but only at a rapidly increasing cost; dependence on the major suppliers in both cases became so strong as to amount to an acceptance of the growing interdependence. It is a confirmation that the trend is general and that, very soon after the issue of Mao's succession in China had been settled, the new leadership repudiated Mao's consistent philosophy of self-sufficiency.

Conflict, competition, and co-operation

An important dimension of international relations is found in the dominant modes in which states conduct their international behaviour and engage in interaction. Relations among individuals can take shape according to a variety of patterns; at one extreme they are based upon pure love, as bestowed by the mother upon her child, and at the other upon unmitigated fear and hatred as felt by the caveman confronted with a stranger. Relations among human groups are similar, except that they are never based on pure love and only rarely on pure fear and hatred. The two extreme types of group relations are often called co-operation, where there is no conflict, and fight, where the conflict is so acute that it makes accommodation unthinkable and the elimination of the opponent the only worthwhile objective. The majority of situations fall between these two and may be called competition. There, conflict exists but is not absolute, because it is tempered by some community of interest, and often ends in compromise.

Relations among states are governed both by the nature of states and that of international society. It may be recalled that the main characteristics of states are that they are the supreme form of human organization, that they recognize no superior and that they are governed by self-interest. Accordingly, international society does not exercise authoritative power over them, although it does prescribe certain rules of behaviour. If social progress is measured by the evolution of co-operation and of peaceful means for the resolution of conflicts, international society is still very primitive.

Interstate behaviour exhibits every type of conflict, from constant references to power politics and threats of violence to actual war which, in our century, has become increasingly more dangerous. The logical conclusion of the present situation is that this Hobbesian starting-point could lead to a form of social contract which would bring to an end this unbearable state of affairs.

The ferocious nature of the two World Wars led to several attempts to eliminate violence: the League of Nations Covenant, the Kellogg Pact, many agreements and declarations, and, lately, the United Nations Charter. Although these approaches varied and were interpreted in differing ways, they did not, as a rule, constitute a departure from the fundamental structure of international society of states governed by self-interest. The states have merely accepted the fact that they were so adversely affected by the danger of recurrent wars that this very self-interest demanded that violence should be eliminated, or, as became current in the language of international organization, that 'aggression' should be prevented. The attempts to outlaw violence did not prevent the Second World War. They did not decrease the danger of a third, nuclear war nearly as much as did common sense, prudential reasoning.

The new institutions and methods not only expressed the idea that a fight to the finish, to eliminate the opponent, was undesirable and therefore scarcely thinkable, but also reinforced this idea by institutionalizing it. During the last War, despite the fundamental nature of the Nazi menace, the United Nations did not seriously contemplate the complete and perpetual elimination of Germany from the international scene; neither do the Americans and Russians necessarily aspire to mutual annihilation—they would be satisfied with a change in each other's social and political systems.

The first attempts to eliminate the use of force having failed, men have sought more effective methods of accommodation by analysing more thoroughly the nature of international conflicts. Especially in the late fifties and sixties the Americans developed ingenious although inconclusive studies based on the 'theory of games', and analysed the complexities of the policy of deterrence. The following paragraphs are based on the ideas of a prominent and influential theoretician of deterrence, the Harvard Professor Thomas C. Schelling, in *The Strategy of Conflict*.

The starting-point of his argument is that pure conflict, war to the finish, would be so mutually damaging that limiting warfare to minimize damage, or coercing the other side by threatening war rather than by waging it, has become expedient for both sides and has opened possibilities of accommodation. There is not only mutual opposition but also mutual dependence. Victory in the conflict is not strictly competitive, not necessarily at the cost of the other side. Conflict situations are now essentially bargaining situations, since they combine a divergence of interests with the powerful common interest that the outcome should not be destructive to both sides; success for both sides means the avoidance of war.

In order to transcend the emotional difficulties of the cold war, Thomas Schelling recommends the study of conflict in other, less emotionally charged and less complex relationships. Undoubtedly the combination of conflicting and common interests, although in different proportions, occurs among non-enemies, and deterrence has its place even among friends and allies. In 1956, when the Poles were standing up to the Russians, their attitude was determined by a combination of the physical threat from Russia and their interest in retaining Soviet support which was indispensable for the maintenance of the Communist regime and of the Western Territories acquired from the Germans. When the Americans unsuccessfully tried to force the French to ratify the European Defence Community in 1954, they stressed common strategic interests but also hinted at the possibility of an 'agonizing re-appraisal' in case of failure. Gang-warfare offers an interesting parallel. Like states, outlaws lack enforceable legal systems, constantly invoke the threat of violence, and ultimately engage in it although they have an interest in avoiding it. Hence they provide illustration for such features of the international system as disarmament and disengagement, surprise attack, retaliation and its threat, appeasement and loss of face, or the unreliability of the widespread alliances and agreements.

The great advantage of this analysis lies in its realism; it takes into account both the conflict and the community of interests, as they exist together in life, while at the same time it shifts attention to the more promising elements of community. Provided each side acts rationally and fully understands the situation, not only as it appears to itself but also as it appears to the other side, the chances of accommodation greatly increase. The fact that the Russians translated the major American analyses and thus had an opportunity to become acquainted with all the subtleties of American views, was an important, perhaps indispensable basis for the subsequent detente.

Finally, we speak of co-operation, where the problem lies not only in the identification of common goals and of the methods of reaching them, but also in the achievement of these goals. This interaction, in which no conflict is involved, does not, properly speaking, come into the ambit of politics which centres on conflict and power, but rather into that of administration. But administration is not only the outcome of successful politics but also offers a method of resolving conflict situations, especially when they are not really acute.

If an international agreement about basic goals and methods is ever reached, it will be a sufficient foundation for the establishment of a world government. Obviously we are very remote from such a state of affairs today, but this does not prevent states from co-operating, in the narrower meaning of the word here employed, namely, interacting without conflict. From the establishment of the Geodetic Union in 1864, international organizations have multiplied to thousands, including many inter-governmental ones; many important activities are carried out under the auspices of the United Nations and of its Specialized Agencies. The so-called 'functional co-operation' embraces wide areas of international life, but is completely successful only when it does not affect power relations. Thus the peaceful progress of international postal administration through the Universal Postal Union strongly contrasts with the turbulent relations in the field of telecommunications, first the telegraph and now the radio. The reasons are not far to seek—they lie in the vastly different strategic importance of the two fields.

Although relatively unimportant from the angle of power relations, international functional co-operation is never fully divorced from them. It offers two interesting prospects. First, as institutions multiply and evolve highly complex methods of co-operation, technical difficulties involved in implementing any political agreement are being reduced and no issue is likely to be wrecked by them. Even such a complex problem as phased disarmament which would offer no sizeable advantage to either side during any phase, can be adequately solved, provided the political decision is made. Second, if the network of the slender ties of functional co-operation continues to increase at the present rate, it may eventually resemble the system of threads with which the Lilliputians tied down Gulliver—although singly the individual strands are weak and insignificant, provided they are sufficiently numerous, their total strength may become substantial. It is conceivable that at some future time states will depend on functional international co-operation to satisfy so many minor human needs that eventually the disruption of such co-operation through violence will become unthinkable. This approach to peace need not exclude other approaches.

The problem of power enters into all types of international relations. Wars, competition, and co-operation, all involve power—the first two military power, though in competition it is used only to deter. All three contain non-military elements—a state which is devoid of resources and organization can neither compete nor co-operate successfully with other states. Hence the logical next step is to discuss the meaning of state power.

The nature of national power

All politics, by definition, revolve around the exercise and the pursuit of power, but in international politics power is considerably more in evidence and less circumscribed than in domestic politics, and hence this field is often described as 'power politics'. The word 'power' is used in many connotations—we speak about Great and Small Powers, about the balance of power, etc. The conspicuous role played by power in international relations has led to a school of interpretation centring around it and also to a reaction in the form of a condemnation of power politics, based on the expectation that power can be eliminated and replaced by international institutions. Neither extreme approach is fully satisfactory. Although power does play a central role in international politics, it is fundamentally an instrument for the achievement of national values. International politics is determined not only by the power wielded by the various states but also, or rather, by the values held by these states; the concept of 'national interest' which governs state behaviour is not limited to power considerations alone.

The school of thought seeking to eliminate power is even less realistic. It is based on the historical experiences of the Anglo-Saxon countries in the nineteenth century. In Britain, power relations at that time become obscured by the apparent divorce of economics from politics and by the temporary security of the country which led to the illusion of a rule of law in international society; in the United States aloofness from the game of European power politics was not only an aspiration but a tangible fact. The moralistic condemnation of power stemming from these experiences, and the exaggerated hope that international institutions would replace power politics, could not stand the test of the totalitarian challenge in the thirties.

A more balanced attitude prevails now. It is futile to attempt a moral evaluation of power in the abstract—it can serve both good and evil purposes. Power certainly cannot be done away with. Our problem is not how to try to eliminate it, which would be futile, but how to control it, to confine it within legitimate channels.

Not all the major problems of power in domestic politics require discussion within the international context. That states wield power is accepted as a fact independently of its possible justification through theories of sovereignty derived from God or the people; in the international context, the organic theories explaining power in terms of its function or the ends it is serving ultimately boil down to self-preservation.

It is not easy to explain the meaning of the word 'power'. In the first instance, a distinction must be made between the word as it is employed in various other spheres. In mathematics 'power' is a technical term meaning the product arising from the continued multiplication of a number by itself; in physics it means the rate of transfer of energy, as in work done by an engine; in human relations it is now generally understood as a relational phenomenon, not a thing that one possesses, it denotes *the capacity to produce intended effects*; specifically, political power is not power over nature, a material, or oneself, but *over the minds and actions of other men*.

The concept of 'power' in human relations is too complex to permit the precision with which it can be used in other domains.

Even in inter-personal relations many interconnected elements must be taken into account. Cleopatra's nose is one famous example of the exercise of power—the argument being that, had it not been for Cleopatra's beauty, Antony could have rallied himself and successfully opposed Octavian. But apart from beauty Cleopatra was also endowed with mental and emotional attributes, and her power cannot possibly be understood without an analysis of the whole complex relationship between her and Antony.

In international relations the concept of 'power' tends to be befogged by two fallacies. It is often understood in a predominantly or even exclusively military sense, as power to wage war. This may have been roughly true about the pre-nuclear era, but the definition is obviously inappropriate to our own age when, against the background of mutual deterrence, other, non-military elements of power are increasingly significant. Moreover, whereas military power remains extremely important in relations between *governments*, it is not much use in the now frequent direct appeals to the *people* of other states. Allied with this is the fallacy that power is measurable and quantifiable just because you can add up and compare such things as the numbers of soldiers under arms, the tonnage of battleships, the potential of the steel industry serving war needs, etc.

In order to explain power in international relations in its broadest meaning it is convenient to distinguish between the relations that include an element of coercion and those that do not. In fact it may be advisable to accept, as Professor Harold Sprout does,[1] the military connotations of the term power and to limit it to actions and situations having within them an element of coercion. The other, non-coercive aspects of power can be called 'influence'. It is unfortunate but symptomatic of our preoccupation with coercion that our language lacks a more precise term for these aspects. Perhaps we cannot find it because the coercive and non-coercive elements cannot be clearly separated. Gentle, persuasive diplomacy works much more efficiently if backed by guns and missiles, although these need never be mentioned; coercive elements, if used starkly, are not very useful since they can lead to desperate opposi-

---

[1] H. and M. Sprout, *The Foundations of International Politics*, 1962.

tion. The use of force, actual physical coercion, is not a logical exercise of power. On the contrary, as shown, for instance, by the Soviet intervention in Czechoslovakia in August 1968, it is a manifestation of power being deficient.

State power involves several important elements usually referred to as capabilities, which will be discussed in turn, but these elements do not add up to a full explanation; indeed, the fact that some of them can be quantitatively expressed should not mislead us into thinking of power as a quantifiable entity. The power of states is better understood through their actions than through the analysis of static elements; as the etymological origin of the word in several languages (*dynamis, potentia*) indicates, it has a potential character. Harold Sprout goes so far as to call the combination of the coercive and non-coercive elements 'potential'; Klaus Knorr calls them 'putative' as against actualized power.

It is possible to conceptualize and compare the power of individual states in various ways. Three dimensions seem to be particularly important: *weight* describes the degree to which the policy of the target state is affected; *scope* refers to the functional aspects, the range of issue-areas in which power is effective, e.g. it may be limited to economic or military issues, or it may be comprehensive; *domain* refers to geographical aspects, the regional, subregional, or global scope of power and the number of states and other targets affected.

The point must be made that, although power plays a role in most international transactions and is central in many, it is not an ingredient in all. We speak then of 'non-political' or 'technical' matters. It is often impossible to agree about the political or non-political character of an issue but, nevertheless, the distinction is very important. It was at the centre of the recurrent controversies between the United States and its allies regarding trade with Communist states immediately after the Second World War; trade, if regarded as predominantly technical, non-political, is governed by quite different considerations from trade considered as political, as a factor which can strengthen a hostile state.

It is the will of states alone that determines the political character of issues. Anything which can even remotely affect the vital interests of the state is political. When it becomes the subject of an international dispute, the state refuses to regard the dispute as legal, i.e. suitable for being decided by an impartial arbiter; it reserves the right to secure terms of settlement which are acceptable to itself, in the last resort even by force. The character of activities does not fully determine their non-political nature even when they are so obviously humanitarian as the abolition of slavery or of forced labour, or protection of human rights in general; they become pronouncedly political when directed against a specific state as happened with the debate over the implementation in the Soviet Union of the obligations regarding human rights under the Final Act of the Helsinki Conference in 1975. The identity of the states involved is just as important as the character of the activity. Obviously Switzerland is much less likely than the United States or the Soviet Union to regard her trade issues as political; furthermore, Swiss trade with a small neutral country like Eire is less likely to give rise to political issues than her trade with one of the Superpowers.

All the analytical categories employed in the discussion of the power of states are fully applicable to that of other international actors. When analysing their international behaviour, we are concerned with the effects of their activities upon the behaviour of other actors, as we are with states. The reasons why traditionally analysis is limited either to states or to non-state actors is found in the difficulties not so much of conceptualization as of the comparison of the actual behaviour of actors which are not fully comparable: their legal positions are different, as only states are sovereign and in control of a territory, and their capabilities lie in different areas. For example, it is very difficult to assess in general terms to what extent the economic power of a multinational corporation can prevail against the political will of a state. The latter may be dependent upon the multinational to sell its minerals, constituting the main source of its income, but may count on the strong support of other radical Third World states. All these factors cannot be readily compared.

Capabilities

Although an analysis of capabilities seems indispensable for the study of international relations, the warning must be repeated that the mechanical sum total of these elements does not take us very far in explaining the actual power potential available to a state. Despite the great progress lately made in statistical analysis, the assessment by Francis Bacon is still applicable:

The greatness of an estate, in bulk and territory, does fall under measure; and the greatness of finances and revenue does fall under computation. The population may appear by musters, and the number of greatness of cities by cards and maps; but yet there is not anything, amongst civil affairs, more subject to error than the right valuation and true judgement concerning the power and forces of an estate.

Power can be realistically estimated only in action, and discussion of capabilities can take us no further than the understanding of the state's potential—or its theoretical capacity for such action.

Some general points should be borne in mind whenever one analyses any particular element of power of any specific state. First, all power elements are relative to those possessed by other states, especially neighbours and possible rivals and opponents. The statement that Britain has a population of some 55 million is meaningless in terms of power-relations unless we compare it with the populations of her larger European neighbours (to which it is roughly equal) and those of the Superpowers (which are much larger). Second, mere quantities are fairly meaningless. Population figures must be broken up according to age, sex, skills, education, etc.; numbers of aeroplanes according to range, speed, weapon-carrying capacity, etc.

Third, single capabilities play their part in the complex totality of the state's power and can be evaluated only against this background. No one element will suffice if the state is deficient in others; for instance, military power alone is inadequate unless it is backed by sufficient population and industrial resources to keep pace with technological advance and to replace possible losses. Thus, with a population of barely seven million people possessing few mechanical skills, Saudia Arabia could not readily become a major military power, despite her lavish expenditure on armaments in the seventies, backed by a commanding position among oil exporters and enormous financial resources. Whenever a state has a surplus of an element of power, over and above actual and likely future needs, this surplus is only marginally relevant as a remote strategic reserve. Thus the United States is not rendered much stronger by the capacity of its steel production, well above its military and civilian needs. The large numbers of China's or India's populations are in one way an element of strength but in another of weakness, since neither country can adequately feed them. In fact, what is usually an element of power can become a liability—for instance if a state deficient in other elements possesses large deposits of rare minerals, e.g. fissionable materials, which make it a coveted prize for the Great Powers.

Fourth, capabilities may be utilized either more or less efficiently. It is conceivable, though not quite certain, that, although Soviet steel production both in absolute quantities and *per capita* is lower than that of the United States, it may be equally adequate for maintaining the Soviet power-position because Soviet consumer industry needs are considerably lower. The power-value of a detachment of troops or weapons varies according to the strategic doctrine they are serving; thus during the Nazi attack on France in May 1940, a tank in the hands of the German Command was strategically much more valuable than a mechanically equivalent tank in the hands of the French.

Fifth, since we live in an area of uniquely rapid technological advance, the relative importance of the various capabilities is constantly changing. Oil has replaced coal as the main source of energy and may itself be replaced in the future by uranium; uranium will lose its value if nuclear processes are mastered to the point of releasing energy through fusion in which only very limited fissionable material is necessary. Weapons are incessantly going out of date—submarines have rendered useless capital ships and ballistic missiles have gone a long way towards supplanting manned aeroplanes. It is not only technology that changes. A profound disturbance in power-relations can arise not only from the evolution of new raw materials or of new weapons but also from the less tangible though equally important changes in the efficiency of government or in the morale of the people.

Sixth, the aspect of readiness must not be neglected. Even in the past all strategists readily distinguished between soldiers actually under arms (forces in being) and soldiers who had to be mobilized, or between operational ships and those laid up. Today, in the era of push-button warfare, there is an even greater difference between a bomber which requires a few hours to be made ready for flying, a bomber kept on the alert, and one actually airborne. The first would be valueless in a surprise attack, and the value of the airborne bomber would be obviously much higher than that of one merely on the alert which, through numerous causes, may not become operational in time.

Consequently analysis should be limited to the data available on the present or the recent past but must perforce include an estimate of trends both in the elements of power currently considered important and in those likely to become so in the future. Here the main problem is how to make the necessary distinctions between reliable statistics and estimates, and between their timing. For example, if we compute the Soviet productive capacity of nuclear missiles, we still do not know how many missiles it has actually produced, since they may not be able or willing to use their capacity to the full. While most strategic analyses centre around inter-continental ballistic missiles, the destructive power of biological and chemical weapons is not compared; simultaneously the 'obsolete' manned bombers still play a significant strategic role. A comparison of the American and the Soviet nuclear striking abilities in 1950, 1960, 1970, and 1980 would produce vastly different results; therefore any comparison must employ statistics and estimates strictly comparable in time.

Population

Undoubtedly the power of a state is related to the size of its population. Although the correlation is not absolute, it is valid to the extent that no state with a small population can become a great Power. The two Superpowers have very large populations, the Soviet Union nearly 260 million and the United States nearly 220 million; the most populous states, China with possibly over 900 million, and India with over 600 million, are serious aspirants to Great Power status although they do not in any way approximate the power-position of the two less populous Superpowers. The sudden growth of the population of Western Europe, especially of Britain, in the last three centuries, had led to the establishment of colonial empires but, in the different conditions of our century, a similar expansion of the populations of Latin America, Asia, and Africa cannot possibly lead to comparable results. An estimate of the trends in population development is indispensable for making long-range power calculations. The highly industrialized Western states, which have reached a fairly stable equilibrium between the birth- and the death-rates, are likely to increase within the next few decades at a very much slower rate than other societies in which the death-rates are being suddenly reduced, although the birth-rates continue high.

Bare numbers do not tell us nearly enough. We must ascertain the proportion of the population in the crucial age-group of 20–50 years, which is both the most productive and the best capable of bearing arms. Comparison of this age-group in different countries requires further refinements according to the utilization of women for both tasks. Whereas during the last War the Soviet Union employed women in industrial production and to some extent also for military service, the Germans did not; hence the correct comparison is that of German manpower and Soviet man- plus 'woman-power'. Furthermore, the extent of literacy, education, and industrial skills can prove decisive. In 1942 the Germans could challenge the Russians because the population of the Soviet Union, although three times more numerous, was inferior to them in most of these respects. Today, this being much less so, the sheer weight of Russian numbers makes such a challenge less thinkable.

Geography

Geography is so prominent in the make-up of the territorial state that some thinkers belonging to the school of 'geopolitics' have been seeking the full explanation of foreign policy in geographical influences. Needless to say, like any other explanation which attempts to reduce a complex reality to the effects of one single factor, 'geopolitics' cannot be accepted as an adequate theory even though the geographical element of power count for much.

Undoubtedly a certain correlation between power and the size of the state's territory does exist, although it is considerably less pronounced than the correlation with the size of the population. The largest state, the Soviet Union, which measures over 8½ million square miles, is very powerful but not more so than the United States which covers just under 3 million. Despite her small area (just over 100,000 square miles when including the whole of Ireland) Britain managed to play a leading role in world politics for a considerable time and to build up the greatest colonial empire. In fact, where vast waste tracts of land divide the centres of population, size can be a handicap until adequate communications have been developed; Australia, for example, is not strengthened by the extensive but barren waste of her interior.

Shape, location, and topography are all important. For strategic and administrative purposes a state should be compact with a capital more or less in the centre, as France is, whereas an elongated state like Czechoslovakia is difficult both to defend and to govern. The 'geopoliticians' have attributed to location a decisive influence, and indeed much of the turbulent history of Germany or Poland is due to their respective positions in the midst of the Central European Plain, whereas, in her insular isolation, Britain was able to develop the foundations of a world empire, while, being located on peripheries, Spain and Portugal, the Scandinavian countries or Japan, sometimes effectively withdrew from the mainstream of power politics. Modern technology has reduced the significance of topography and the desirability of such 'natural frontiers' as mountain-ranges or rivers, but location remains important.

Finally, climate greatly influences the produce of the land and the character of its people. The great centres of power have so far arisen only in the moderate zone, between twenty and sixty degrees North.

Economics

The economic basis of modern states is paramount both in peace and war. It determines the living conditions and the well-being of their peoples and provides them with the wherewithal for a successful foreign policy; it also serves as the foundation for an armaments industry and can be regarded as ultimately decisive in war.

The Gross National Product (G.N.P.) is useful as a general index of economic strength particularly when supplemented by a break-down on the *per capita* basis and by an estimate of the growth rate. Unfortunately national figures are computed in different ways and are therefore not strictly comparable.

Usually two components are distinguished in the economic element: natural resources and industrial production. Again comparisons are inaccurate but nevertheless quite telling as general indicators of strength.

Whenever evaluating the economic elements of power one must

bear in mind the distinction between capacity and actual production. Although the Soviet steel production capacity is smaller than that of the United States, it is generally more fully utilized while, owing to economic fluctuations, the American capacity is generally worked only partly; hence the discrepancy between the quantities of steel actually produced by the two countries is considerably less than that between their capacities. Moreover, while much of American steel is put to a marginally social use, for instance to make the cars even bigger, it is for power purposes much less effectively used than Soviet steel which is made into weapons and essential consumer goods. Against that, the quality of the product must be borne in mind; defective end-products which are useless or only partially useful are likely to be produced less frequently in the competitive American system than in a Communist society where dire penalties threaten factories which fail to produce their allotted quotas, regardless of quality.

If a state is deficient in a raw material or productive capacity, one must investigate how it can overcome the shortage through stockpiling or imports, and on what economic and strategic conditions, or how a substitute could be discovered through technological advance. For instance, one of the strategically important materials which the United States lacks is rubber. For a long time the Americans were dependent on imports from South-east Asia, which put them into a strategically dangerous position owing to the distances involved; to meet a sudden emergency they stockpiled considerable quantities of rubber and finally they evolved methods of producing artificial rubber which is in some respects superior to the natural product. The process is, however, slow, not only in actual life but even in conceptualizing it. For instance, in the seventies the world was faced with an 'energy crisis', owing to the rapidly growing energy needs and even more rapidly growing dependence upon oil imports to satisfy them. After a lapse of many years it was not, however, clear what this meant in computing the power of states. On the one hand, the dominant position of Saudi Arabia as not only the leading oil exporter but also the only exporter capable of a rapid further massive increase in its supplies, was not translated into a position of clear diplomatic influence; on the other, the growing dependence of the United States on oil imports and particularly on Saudi Arabia was not directly translated into a loss of diplomatic influence—the resulting substantial imbalance in payments and the weakness of the dollar were very much more significant. In the mutual relations of Saudi Arabia and the United States the former did not manage to use her advantage to really good effect to prevent the latter from continuing to extend protection to the state of Israel. In the longer run, however, a greater degree of such influence could be anticipated.

Only the two Superpowers approached self-sufficiency, but only for a while, and even then they were dependent on the importation of some raw materials. In 1960 the United States imported some seventy key materials totalling about fifteen per cent of its entire raw material consumption, and it was estimated that these imports would rise further. The Soviet Union imports considerably less and is more likely to find at home additional raw materials to meet the needs of increased industrial production in the future. In the late seventies, the United States became a large-scale oil importer, and the Soviet Union, too, was facing the prospect of becoming one.

Strategically important raw materials fall into three groups with a certain overlap: fuels (coal, oil, natural gas, and fissile materials); metals (especially iron to which coal must be added for steel production; copper; metals used to harden steel such as chromium, manganese, and nickel; bauxite, lead, zinc, tin, titanium, silver, etc.); and agricultural produce, subdivided into food and industrial crops. In industrial production, steel output, which is the basis of all heavy industry and particularly of the production of weapons, usually receives much prominence; the chemical and the electronics industries are now important in all advanced economies.

Clearly, the two Superpowers lead the world and are matched only by Japan and by the E.E.C. which, however, is only loosely organized. A number of other states are, however, seriously set on the path of industrialization: some of them are small, like South Korea or Taiwan, but some are big, like Brazil or India. Moreover, economic growth has now become the major goal of all states which are appropriately referred to in this context as 'under-developed', 'less-developed', or 'developing'. From the point of view of power-relations, states already industrialized are in a much better position than others. Not only can they supply more weapons for their armies and more goods for their people, but they have a much better chance of crossing the threshold beyond which economic growth becomes a self-perpetuating process, as it is in the West and in the Soviet Union. In the longer run, however, as more and more producers compete for raw materials, although greater deposits of these are constantly found and more efficiently exploited and although substitutes often become possible, it is conceivable that states controlling rare crucial raw materials will be in the most powerful position, able to command in exchange all that they require. This has already happened with oil.

Government and military organization

The potential elements of power are utilized according to how efficiently they are organized; hence the importance of government. Sudden changes in the power position of a state can be entirely due to a change of government, as happened in Germany, when the Nazis replaced the Weimar Republic, or in China, when Communist Government replaced a demoralized Nationalist one.

The contemporary types of authoritarian and democratic governments differ in their respective advantages and disadvantages. An authoritarian government can override the wishes of its people and hence can act with speed, and, at least in the short run, with efficiency. A democratic government must persuade its people first. This is often a slow and difficult process, sometimes to no avail, but it has the off-setting advantage that the more active consent of the people ensures the stability of the government and enables it to withstand stress. If we compare the systems in contemporary China and India, we find that the Chinese Government was the more able to mobilize the whole population and to divert scarce resources to economic development but became involved in a devastating 'Cultural Revolution'. The much less efficient and less ruthless Indian Government may have done quite as well although it continues to face severe economic and minority challenges.

How significant is the quality of the civil service, is demonstrated by the comparison of newly emancipated colonial territories. Countries which inherited a reasonable civil service, such as Ghana or Nigeria, fared, at least at first, much better than countries in which it had broken down, as Indonesia or the Belgian Congo. For international relations, particularly relevant is the quality of diplomacy.

Although, as has been mentioned, its role is often exaggerated, military power is an essential condition for the survival of the state in war and also in peacetime, to enable it to pursue policies of effective deterrence and to endow the state with the capabilities necessary for the making of an effective ally. Comparisons of military organization are confusing since we must bear in mind at least three separate military elements: the strategic deterrent; the so-called conventional weapons, traditionally divided into air, naval, and army branches; and the strategic doctrine. Moreover, the respective importance of the three is constantly changing. During the immediate post-war years the Americans greatly over-rated nuclear weapons to the detriment of conventional ones. Even now possession of nuclear weapons is a major condition for Great Power status, and nuclear equilibrium is the major objective of the two Superpowers. As Britain is closely associated with the United States, her nuclear weapons constitute no major problem as do those possessed by France and China. Quite a few additional states possess, however, the technological ability to produce nuclear weapons and some of them may have actually done so. As despite international negotiations the prospects of an effective prevention of nuclear proliferation are not very promising, the effect on the global and on regional power balances is bound to be fundamental. This has already happened in the Middle East and in South Asia as Israel and India are likely to have actually produced nuclear weapons.

The value of strategic doctrine lies in choosing military power of the right kind. Thus French military doctrine in the inter-war period can be blamed for the defeat in 1940, since the French were prepared for a static trench warfare of the First World War type and not for the mobile warfare of the Second World War, imposed upon them by the attacking Germans. Today the major problems lie in determining the proportion of resources to be devoted to nuclear weapons necessary for deterrence and for a nuclear war, and to conventional weapons useful in minor conflicts. Also the differences between the strategy of deterrence and that to be employed in the minor clashes of the cold war, such as subversion or infiltration, require definition.

The proportion of the G.N.P. devoted to military ends indicates the intensity of the military effort and offers a clue to the prospects of its durability. In 1976 the Russians devoted to it some 11–13 per cent of their G.N.P., the Americans only some 6 per cent. The latter, additionally, not only enjoy a much higher national product, but also do not fully utilize their industrial capacity. Hence sustained or even increased armament programmes would not be particularly onerous for them; on the contrary, they would mean a more efficient use of facilities and less unemployment. The Russians, by contrast, are showing definite signs of economic strain. It is obvious that they could very usefully employ a large proportion of their defence expenditure for urgent investment needs and consumption.

Comparison of actual military strength is highly technical and need not be pursued here beyond the conclusion that both the Americans and the Russians have more than sufficient 'second-strike capability', i.e. enough nuclear weapons to inflict 'unacceptable' damage on the opponent even after having been subject to a devastating nuclear attack; the power-value of the British and the French deterrents is highly controversial. Likewise inconclusive is the comparison of conventional military resources. While we can count the troops and weapons classified according to their striking power, the intangible element of the political attitudes of both the soldiers and the civilians must not be neglected. Support, although often enforced, of the native people for Communist guerrillas in South-east Asia multiplied the power-value of the numerically small active Communists; nationalist, anti-Russian sentiments may greatly reduce the reliability and hence the power-value of the Warsaw Pact troops; certainly the Czech troops could scarcely be expected to fight whole-heartedly.

Psychological-social elements

This category embraces all the less tangible elements of power which cannot be easily bracketed within any of the preceding categories.

It is necessary to distinguish the social system from the governmental one. A people united and homogeneous are obviously much stronger than one disunited and heterogeneous. Any major rifts, whether racial, national, religious, or of any other kind, detract, at least potentially, from the power of the state because it may not be able to muster the whole strength of its population whenever factional interests clash. This somewhat intangible element used to augment the power of the United Kingdom while its social system remained stable. It casts doubts on the ultimate strength of the Soviet Union where important national, religious, and ideological differences clearly exist. While they lasted, the racial disturbances in the United States seriously detracted from its power potential.

Then there is the factor often referred to as morale. Morale describes the extent to which the people support their leaders, believe in the future of their state and in the rightness of their cause. It depends upon a combination of circumstances and the quality of leadership and can be subject to frequent and sometimes sudden fluctuations. Thus the French morale was much higher than the British throughout the sixties but was severely shaken by the students' riots and the general strike in 1968.

A more permanent intangible element is national character. Although the stereotypes of national character can be grossly misleading, there is some foundation for the observation that different nations tend to develop their own peculiar ways of thinking and acting, some of which are more useful than others for the power of the state; there can be little doubt about the advantages of German industriousness or the disadvantages of Polish unruliness in the past. Analysis of national character does not, however, take us very far. First of all, national character, although much more stable than morale, does change. In the seventeenth century the English were reputed to be the most turbulent nation in Europe and in the eighteenth the Germans the most romantic and peaceful, but quite justifiably neither reputation holds today. Second, it is notoriously difficult to agree on what national character actually is or how useful are some of its features. It is fairly easy to catalogue the differences between the Americans and the Russians and to arrive at the conclusion that their national characters are diametrically opposed. It is not much more difficult to list the similarities due to the common factors of size and concentration on material achievements, and to arrive at the opposite conclusion.

Prestige is derived from some features of society that involve power and from others that do not, but is an element of power in itself because it helps the state to obtain the desired social response from others. Prestige is built upon the image formed by others of the state's qualities, an image often having little in common with reality—especially when the supposed qualities are merely a matter of the past. The qualities that count for the purpose of prestige vary from period to period, and states tend to evolve their own individual methods for enhancing their reputations.

Military, today particularly nuclear power, is a sound foundation for international prestige. So is economic strength, though here prestige ambiguously embraces several elements: there is the element of economic strength as a basis for and supplement to military power, as the ability to provide largesse abroad, and as a testimony to the soundness of the ideological foundations of society. In the latter respect, the Russians used to be able to score because their centrally planned economy could boast of one of the highest rates of economic growth sustained over many years. One should not, however, forget the frequently unacknowledged prestige accruing to the United States for its indisputably high standard of living and for all the glossy gadgets its citizens enjoy. Despite all the incidental harm Hollywood films may have been doing to American prestige, they ensure that the whole world is familiar with the American standard of living.

In our age which is so acutely aware of human rights, social justice has become important for the reputation of states. Especially since 1975, as the protection of human rights has now become a legally recognized international concern under the Final Acts of the Helsinki Conference, infringements of such rights when dealing with ideological dissidents have become seriously damaging to the Soviet Union. Particularly obnoxious is racial discrimination which accounts for the extreme diplomatic isolation of South Africa, a country pursuing her policy of separate development of races, the apartheid, despite international opprobrium.

International strategic position

State power is determined not only by the combination of all the above-mentioned domestic elements of power but also by the position of the state in the world. No state, not even the Superpowers, is fully self-supporting; all depend on military allies, on friends in diplomacy, on suppliers and markets in trade. All the elements of power in their possession can be considerably augmented by outside support. Such support is highly desirable, perhaps indispensable, but its value and cost require careful computation. Although numerical precision cannot be achieved, it seems to be useful to think about international support as a kind of multiplier—positive or negative—to domestic capabilities. On issues of development of anti-colonialism or racialism, any new, developing state can count on sustained support of the Group of 77 and usually also of Communist states so that its capabilities, however slender, are accordingly augmented. By contrast, a state faced with international opprobrium must discount its national capabilities accordingly; for quite different individual reasons, this is the case with South Africa, Israel, and Taiwan. Hence these are sometimes bracketed as 'pariah states', however heterogeneous this category is in all other significant respects.

Foreign support is not very reliable. The ultimate command of the resources which can be called upon from abroad remains in foreign hands: the promised troops may be refused at the last minute, the expected economic aid may be stopped, the raw materials may not be delivered. Excessive reliance on uncertain support is obviously dangerous. Moreover, there are the drawbacks of cost and risk. The concessions necessary to ensure the reliability of an ally may be so great as to reduce the power of the state in relation to this ally, although the alliance strengthens its power in relation to other states. To take the example of American alliances since the last War—they certainly have proved costly and are, with the exception of NATO, usually both ineffective and precarious. While they have been concluded and are being maintained in the belief that they increase American power, the contrary could be argued about alignments such as that with South Vietnam, which directly led to American involvement in the Vietnam War.

The value of political support short of an alliance, or of benevolent neutrality, is obvious in the deliberations of the General Assembly. The United States and the Soviet Union vie in their efforts to secure the goodwill of the numerically preponderant Afro-Asian bloc; much of Soviet diplomatic power in the United Nations comes from the anti-colonial and therefore anti-Western attitudes of this bloc. A state concerned in a matter coming up on the agenda of the General Assembly is compelled to make the rounds of other members, and the isolation of such states as South Africa or Israel greatly reduces their power.

7 Instruments and techniques of state interaction

Some general distinctions

Two important but necessary limitations of the subsequent discussion must be noted in advance. First, the whole of the contemporary international system is dealt with in all its great variety and in its broad historical setting; consequently analysis can be neither very full nor very precise. Second, it is limited to the forms of direct state interaction. A legitimate objection against such a delimitation could be raised on the grounds that often what is in form a purely domestic policy can profoundly affect other states—e.g. the economic or the armaments programme of the United States. It is, however, not unrealistic to assume that any domestic matter with a sufficiently strong international component is bound to be taken up internationally.

In the first instance it is necessary to discuss the degree of choice of instruments and techniques open to individual states. Clearly such choice is limited by the availability of the appropriate capabilities: a state militarily weak is naturally inclined to develop its foreign relations with the aid of non-military instruments and techniques; a state economically weak is limited in its choice of economic instruments and techniques. The choice, however, cannot be made at the will of the state, according to a rational appraisal of its attitudes to the other party and of its power-position. Some inescapable influences arise within the international environment—challenges and opportunities in every field change with the passage of time; international fashions and the 'rules of the game' governing international intercourse are not static. Thus post-war American foreign policy has been justly criticized for its excessive reliance upon nuclear weapons in which the United States was strong, despite the fact that these weapons are useless in most situations and that the major Communist challenges have gradually shifted to the ideological and the economic fields. France and Britain learnt only through the failure of their Suez expedition in 1956 that in the mid-twentieth century armed intervention could be undertaken only with the support of at least one of the Superpowers or of the United Nations. For some years the Western Powers were rather pathetically complaining that they could not cope with Communist-inspired subversion.

Attempts at disarmament, an agreed reduction of the military instruments, would be clearly in the general interest. Not only would all states save colossal sums of money on an increasingly costly item of expenditure but also the instruments of violence would be limited and hence external threats would be reduced. This is the origin of disarmament proposals which started with the initiative of the Russian Tsar at the end of the last century and have continued into the SALT talks between the Superpowers in the seventies. The results were not encouraging and rarely went beyond platitudinous declarations of the need to agree to a disarmament scheme. While the rationale of disarmament from the systemic point of view is clear, that from the point of view of the individual states is beset with fears and uncertainties about the possible effects of any concrete scheme. Disarmament attempts are supplemented by attempts to outlaw war which culminate in the far-reaching prohibition of the use or threat of force in the conduct of international relations; it is embodied in the Charter of the United Nations, is not always observed but exercises some influence on the behaviour of states. In general, other things not being too unequal, states will tend to choose instruments and techniques compatible with the Charter and likely to find approval with international public opinion as expressed in the General Assembly. Of course the degree of deference varies with the single states and according to the significance of the issues involved.

The choice of instruments and techniques by an individual state cannot be fully divorced from the determination of foreign policy as a whole. Some variables can, however, be singled out as being particularly relevant for choices. To start with, there is the very fundamental issue of the *intensity* of international relations which greatly varies in different areas and periods.

While Mesopotamia became the stage of ramified international relations some millennia before our era, the remote Himalayan realms of Tibet and Nepal remained isolated until this century. One cannot appreciate the foreign policy of any state without some idea of how involved it is in its relations with other states—today the United States and the Soviet Union are obviously the most active countries, while many neutrals are trying with varying degrees of success to stay out of the mainstream of power politics. Major issues of foreign policy centre around involvement, for instance to what extent should Britain or France pursue their policies as nuclear powers, as active members of NATO, and as senior partners in networks of relationships with their ex-colonies?

Traditionally, states have been trying to escape what they considered excessive involvement through isolationism and neutrality. Isolationism, meaning a deliberate withdrawal from international relations, is no longer possible on the basis of geographical isolation, as pursued by China and Japan until the relatively recent incursion of European influence. Britain's 'splendid isolation' in the nineteenth century did not really amount to non-involvement; on the contrary, Britain actively participated in all major European conflicts except the Franco-Prussian War. The term merely described the operation of the balance of power system which did not demand from Britain continuous participation but only sporadic interventions. Likewise the 'splendid isoltion' of the United States was to some extent mythical. The Americans were extremely active in the Western Hemisphere and closely watched European politics but, owing to the protection of the friendly British Navy, they could refrain from taking part in them directly.

Fifty years ago neutrality was primarily a strictly legal concept describing non-participation in war, which confers certain rights and imposes certain duties on the neutral states. The United States in the First World War until its entry or Eire in the Second World War are recent examples. Although more rarely, the concept applied also to more broadly political orientations in peacetime such as the neutralization of Belgium in 1939 or the traditional policies of the classical European neutrals, Switzerland and Sweden. In response, however, to the nuclear weapons and the cold war, under the new name of 'non-alignment' neutrality has spread very widely since 1945, especially among the new states. Its basic meaning consists of not being committed to either major bloc and of refusing to participate in their systems of alliances. The term applies to a state's attitude to the cold war alone. The non-aligned states endeavour to avoid commitment to either the Russians or the Americans but they are, in varying degrees, involved in quite intensive international relations outside this context. Moreover, some individual non-aligned states come under the strong influence of one of the Superpowers so that their neutrality is by no means even-handed. Ever since its foundation at the Bandung Conference in 1945 the non-aligned bloc has been a major feature of the international system, but its continuation requires consummate diplomatic skills and manoeuvres on the part of its leaders. In 1978 it came under a particularly severe strain owing to the dispute over the large-scale Cuban military interventions in Africa.

Another important variable is *crisis* perception. Definitions of a 'crisis' vary but, according to most writers, it is a situation characterized by high levels of threat to some vital interest, according to some, including a high probability of military activities; by time-pressure resulting in decision-making generally being conducted higher up the hierarchy and in an accelerated—which inevitably means also simplified—manner; and often also by surprise. Thus, by definition, crisis situations result in a strong bias towards the use of the military instrument and of force. Hence, both from the systemic and from the individual state's point of view it is important to conceive of methods of crisis management and containment which would be as effective as possible.

General attitudes to the stability of the international order constitute another important variable. Some states like to preserve stability which, they feel, serves their national interest; they are the defenders of the *status quo* (*status quo ante bellum* is a legal term describing in peace treaties the state of affairs which had existed before the beginning of hostilities); others, feeling that the order is against their national interest and that they would gain by changing it, are usually described as *revisionist* powers. These positive or negative attitudes to the existing international order vary in intensity and determination. Not all supporters of the *status quo* are equally ready to defend it, and, likewise, not all revisionist states are equally determined to strive for the downfall of the existing order. Moreover, states vary greatly in their attitudes to friends, potential enemies, and neutrals. Inevitably they are influenced by these in their choice of instruments and techniques.

In the interaction among states there are no clear-cut divisions between friends and foes, between persuasion and coercion. In most cases relations include varying, even conflicting, elements—a threat of coercion occasionally creeps into the most amicable relationship and even ardent ideological opponents may find it possible to compromise in matters of trade. Peace does not preclude the existence of conflict, even of quite an acute nature, nor does war mean complete severance of non-coercive relations. All the instruments and techniques of international intercourse have some application both in friendly and in hostile relations, in peace and in war, even though some are pronouncedly more persuasive while others are pronouncedly more coercive.

Until the First World War international relations were conducted with other governments alone, but since then relations with the people of other states or other sub-groups have been growing in importance. Consequently instruments and techniques suitable for inter-governmental relations have been supplemented and to a certain extent displaced by those suitable for approaching these people. Often dilemmas arise. For instance, when determining their relations with unfriendly Communist governments in Eastern Europe immediately after 1945, the Americans sometimes helped them in their economic difficulties in the hope of securing their goodwill and weakening their allegiance to the Soviet bloc (this was called detachment). The alternative was to appeal to the people of these countries to overthrow their governments and replace them with governments which would be more friendly to the United States and would therefore qualify for assistance (this was called subversion). Obviously these two policies are incompatible.

Foreign policy is not only directed towards other governments but can also use them as instruments. One of the characteristics of the post-war period has been 'aggression by proxy'. The Russians used their own troops only in neighbouring countries. The many Communist-inspired and supported actions and disturbances which took place elsewhere immediately after the war were conducted by foreign Communists employed as instruments of Soviet foreign policy; only the Yugoslav and the Chinese revolutions were genuinely national. Military intervention by proxy remained in use in the late seventies when it was undertaken on a large scale by Cuban troops in Angola and on the Horn of Africa, with the

Russians providing only military supplies and transport.

The various instruments and techniques will be analysed according to the fields within which they operate. A large proportion of state behaviour is verbal and falls within two categories known as diplomacy and propaganda, while economic and military activities are of central importance and show specific characteristics.

Diplomacy

The word 'diplomacy' is often employed in a broad meaning which embraces both the making and the execution of foreign policy. In its more technical meaning here employed it has been aptly described as the business of communicating between governments. It is the inevitable outcome of the coexistence of separate political units with any degree of contact and, indeed, its origins can be traced to remote antiquity. Greece, Byzantium, and Renaissance Italy made the most notable contributions to the evolution of contemporary diplomacy. At all times rulers considered diplomacy an important instrument of state policies but gradually it transcended a purely national role. Although the diplomats were governed exclusively by the dictates of national policy and ruthlessly employed cunning, deceit, and duplicity, as realistically described by Machiavelli in *The Prince*, they slowly evolved a certain orderliness of procedure. In the eighteenth century the common interest in the maintenance of an international equilibrium led to a fundamental reorganization. The balance of power system, which will be discussed in the following chapter, fundamentally affected the conduct of diplomacy. It demanded constant vigilance from its participants and hence diplomatic missions became permanent instead of sporadic. This, in turn, led to the consolidation of diplomatic procedures and practices which was facilitated by the common aristocratic origin of the practitioners and by the common interest in the existing international order; in 1815, after the end of the Napoleonic Wars, the process was formalized by the regulations of Aix-la-Chapelle.

Thus the interest in international order shared by all states transformed the nature of diplomacy. Since the national interests of the several states could not be successfully secured except through the maintenance of the balance of power, diplomacy had to serve the requirements of the system as a whole. Instead of the intrigues and deceit prevalent earlier in history, the qualities of integrity, good faith, and honest negotiation became increasingly stressed. While remaining a major instrument of state policy, diplomacy became also a major agency operating on behalf of international society.

The golden age of diplomacy passed together with the balance of power system and, following the fundamental changes in international society since 1918, we entered an era of what is often called popular or new diplomacy. One fundamental reason for this was the transformation of technology and communications. Already in 1919 the actual heads of the governments of the Allied and Associated Powers spent long periods together, deliberating over the Peace Treaty with Germany. Since then, the evolution of aeroplanes and telecommunications has greatly increased the speed of diplomacy and therefore has reduced the importance of the diplomats in the field; to a large extent diplomacy now overlaps with policy-making. Moreover, new means of mass-communication have opened the means of direct approach to the people of other countries through propaganda. This not only detracts from the importance of diplomacy but sometimes conflicts with its basic purpose as well as with its day-to-day operation.

Moreover, in the West, public opinion has forcibly intruded into the conduct of foreign policy and has weakened the esteem in which diplomacy had been formerly held. The people were suspicious of power politics and of the balance of power system which had led to the 1914–18 War; hence they suspected diplomacy as the major instrument of foreign policy and attacked its traditional secrecy. President Wilson, the most influential spokesman of the new view, formulated the ideal in the very first of his famous Fourteen Points:

Open covenants of peace, openly arrived at, after which there shall be no private international understandings of any kind, but diplomacy shall proceed always frankly and in the public view.

Open diplomacy means two things—first, that there should be no secret agreements; second, that negotiations should be in the open. While the former condition is reasonable and is firmly rooted in democratic theory, the latter has proved embarrassing. Once the diplomats state their national demands in public, they generally cannot agree to a compromise without loss of face; in other words, they cannot effectively negotiate.

The composition of international society has now completely changed. Europe is no longer the exclusive centre of international affairs and, since the last War, power has become concentrated in the hands of two non-European states, the United States and the Soviet Union. The numbers of the members of international society have swollen with the emancipation of colonial territories in Asia and in Africa; the new states are much more remote from European diplomatic traditions than even the two Superpowers.

Moreover, the United Nations has become an important supplementary and, to some extent, competitive channel for international intercourse, some of which is conducted in the traditional manner by the diplomatic representatives to the United Nations whose private negotiations are particularly useful to states which do not maintain direct diplomatic relations. However, the United Nations also represents a new dimension in diplomacy, sometimes called diplomacy by conference, or by parliamentary procedures, or forensic diplomacy. This diplomacy is conducted openly in conferences or assemblies, and, instead of the art of compromise, its requires the art of persuasion to secure the votes of as many members as possible. Since the egalitarian nature of international organization ensures one vote for each state, the wooing of many becomes essential.

Finally, instead of operating within a fairly stable international society based upon the operation of a balance of power in which all the members were interested, diplomacy today operates in a world in which the rival blocs are rent by ideological rifts and have only limited common interests. While the new states are interested mainly in economic growth and in preserving their newly won independence from entanglements, the Communist and the Western blocs continue to suspect each other's intentions. Although it is logical to assume that both share a vital interest in the continuation of the present balance and in the prevention of the spread of nuclear weapons which could upset this balance, the implications of this common interest have not as yet been fully absorbed by diplomacy.

The organization of the diplomatic machinery has remained

unaltered ever since the beginning of the nineteenth century but, owing to the multiplication of state units, only the Superpowers can maintain separate diplomatic relations with nearly all of them. Provided no difficulties of recognition arise, most states exchange diplomatic missions only with the Superpowers, with neighbours, and with other states with which they have much business. These missions are either embassies headed by ambassadors or, less frequently and on a lower ceremonial level, legations headed by ministers. Whereas in the nineteenth century ambassadorial status was granted less frequently—only to important Powers—nowadays it has become more a mark of good relations and an expression of goodwill. The chief functions of diplomacy remain the protection of the interests of the country and of its citizens abroad, representing (legal, symbolic, and social) observation, reporting, and most importantly, negotiation.

Negotiations cover an extremely wide range of international transactions and can be conducted in various ways—by the ambassador of a country in the capital of another, or by its foreign ministry in its own capital; heads of government or foreign ministers engage in 'summit diplomacy' or use their personal agents; diplomatic representatives accredited to the United Nations or to a third country may be in charge, especially if the two countries have no direct diplomatic relations; special international conferences may be convened. Negotiations may be formal, conducted through an exchange of notes, or informal, through personal, sometimes unofficial contacts. The basic objective of all negotiations is to obtain from other states consent to what is considered to be in the national interest—it may be an agreement on limitation of armaments, or support in the General Assembly of the United Nations, or the conclusion of a trade agreement, or protection of the interests of nationals living in the other state, or anything else which may be quite vital or merely trivial. Negotiations necessarily begin with an exchange of statements of the views of both parties and consist essentially of bargaining, of seeking a compromise between these views. Areas of mutual agreement are defined and as far as possible enlarged, areas of disagreement are defined and as far as possible reduced through mutual compromise until accord is reached. This may be entirely informal or it may be embodied in a formal international treaty.

When the parties are basically antagonistic, negotiations are conducted not with the usual purpose of securing agreement but to damage the position of an opponent and to express hostility. It happened in the past, for instance, when the Chinese were negotiating with Lord Napier at Canton in 1830 or when the Russian Bolsheviks met the Germans at Brest Litovsk in 1919; it has been happening frequently since 1945 under the impact of the cold war. In spite of their avowed desire to negotiate, the Communists and frequently also the Americans appear to be intractable; possibly during the prolonged negotiations on disarmament neither side ever seriously contemplated or desired a compromise.

Public announcements and behind-the-scenes negotiations do not always coincide. When the Russians and then the Americans resumed nuclear testing in 1962, they accused each other in public of committing crimes against humanity. But, because they wished to prevent other Powers from developing nuclear weapons, these public condemnations did not prevent them from privately seeking an agreement to ban tests, though not before they themselves had completed a further series. Such divergence between public announcements and private behaviour may appear cynical but in fact the two Powers quite reasonably combined vital national interests with propaganda warfare.

In all negotiating it is imperative to save face. For instance, in the Cuban crisis in 1962 President Kennedy forced Khrushchev to withdraw his missiles from Cuba but enabled him to cover up his retreat by undertaking not to invade Cuba. Failing such a face-saving formula Khrushchev might have found a withdrawal impossible.

Disarmament talks under U.N. auspices have been continuing throughout much of the post-war period not in the hope of reaching any substantial agreement but largely because the major parties justifiably wished to avoid the opprobrium of breaking them off.

Normally negotiations are the simplest way for reconciling competing national interests and hence they perform a central function not only in the conduct of the foreign policy of every single state but also in the operation of the international system as a whole. They are invaluable in that they offer the simplest method of peaceful settlement of conflicts; as long as they are continued, the outbreak of violence is less likely. As a rule negotiations deal with concrete issues and details, and parties concentrating on these are diverted from intractable fundamentals with their attendant prejudices and passions.

The basic technique of negotiation is persuasion and compromise. Most issues, however controversial, involve a certain community of interests; when relations between the negotiating parties are fundamentally friendly, persuasion and compromise often suffice. If necessary, inducements have to be offered, either positive, such as military or technical assistance, or negative, such as threats of unpleasant actions, in extreme cases including the threat of force. Different states have developed different national traditions in diplomatic style, and the discrepancies between the Communist and the traditional Western styles continue to impede diplomacy today. Nevertheless quite a successful theory of international bargaining of general application has been developed. It is based on the theory of games, especially on the analysis of threats and promises. The theory is sufficiently flexible to be applicable to bargaining in all situations, e.g. it was useful to the structuring of American/Soviet bargaining both in the conditions of the cold war, when emphasis was laid upon the rational employment of threats and deterrence, and during the subsequent detente, when the emphasis shifted to the dangers inherent in these and consequently to promises.

When mutual attitudes are diffident or hostile and the formulation of an issue or the form of compromise are difficult to reach, sometimes a third party plays a part. It may offer its 'good offices', and bring the two parties together; it may take part in actual negotiations, which is called 'mediation'; it may even participate in the determination of the terms of settlement, which is called 'conciliation'. Even further-reaching is 'arbitration' which means a binding adjudication by impartial arbiters. It was spectacularly successful in the *Alabama* case between Britain and the United States in 1872 and, although it did not rise to the sanguine expectations of its supporters, it still is a potentially significant adjunct to diplomacy. In 1920 a permanent World Court in The Hague was established to further facilitate adjudication.

When successful, negotiations often lead to the conclusion of a formal treaty. The significance of treaties greatly varies, depending upon their subject-matter and the identity of the parties; most important are agreements which lay the foundation for future co-operation on vital matters, such as alliances which are a traditional method of pooling together the power of states with a common political purpose and a common potential enemy. The two important features of alliances are that they can be concluded by states as different as the Western Powers and the Soviet Union during the last war, and that their duration fully depends on the existence of the common enemy.

More permanent are alignments resulting from membership of the international institutions. Normally the treaties concerned provide some method for the termination of the institution or the withdrawal of individual members, but the contemporary tendency is to omit such provisions. The United Nations Charter does not mention them, although discussions before the signature of the treaty confirmed that withdrawal remains open; the European Economic Community is meant to be permanent.

Propaganda

By propaganda we generally understand any systematic attempt to affect the minds, emotions, and actions of a given group for a specific public purpose. While propaganda, like diplomacy, is on the whole verbal, it differs from diplomacy in two important respects. First, it is addressed to the *people* of other states rather than to their *governments* (the important subject of propaganda conducted by the government at home need not concern us here); the effect on other governments is rarely more than incidental.

Second, propaganda is selfish, governed exclusively by the national interests of the propagandist and therefore usually unacceptable to other states. There is here no attempt to find a compromise between competing national interests; the aim is exclusively the national advantage of the propagandist. As far as international order is concerned, propaganda, as it is conducted by the various states, serves purely negative purposes. Not only is it never employed for the purposes of this order as diplomacy occasionally is, but all international efforts to curb at least its most vicious forms have as yet been unavailing.

At the same time the dividing-lines between diplomacy and propaganda are not fully clear-cut. Thus, negotiations sometimes degenerate into exercises in propaganda directed at the public and not at the governments. Moreover, the Russian and the Chinese Communists are cultivating extensive relations with foreign groups sympathetic to their ideology. The most important of these are the Communist parties, but there are also numerous other groups, often called cover-organizations, such as the national units of the World Peace Council, the World Federation of Trade Unions, the World Federation of Democratic Youth, etc. While all these serve the purposes of Communist propaganda, relations with them are conducted on a quasi-diplomatic, although not governmental level.

Propaganda did not play a significant role in international affairs until the 1914–18 War. Previously only the Catholic Church had used it and had institutionalized the propagation of faith through a special Sacred Congregation (*de propaganda fide*) from the title of which the word 'propaganda' is derived. The British Government during the First World War was the first to organize and systematize the use of propaganda at home and abroad. Its efforts abroad were fairly successful in securing the goodwill of the neutrals, especially the Americans, but less so in appealing to the Germans. Other belligerents did not employ propaganda quite as systematically or extensively and the organizations built up during the War disappeared after its end.

The real impetus to the development of propaganda was given by the growth of the totalitarian regimes in the inter-war period. First the Communists and then the Nazis built up tremendous and costly propaganda machines and the Western democracies were gradually forced to match their efforts. Despite the defeat of Nazism, post-war propaganda has further increased in scope. The Russians try to stir up discontent and to secure the allegiance of the people in the West while the Americans have parallel aims regarding the people of the Communist bloc. Equally important are the competing appeals of both to the peoples and also the governments of the uncommitted countries. Agencies which are in charge of these propaganda activities, the United States Central Information Agency (C.I.A.) and the Agitation and Propaganda Section of the Central Committee of the Soviet Communist Party, have assumed considerable importance and operate on large budgets. Here, as in the field of armaments, other states find it difficult to compete. For instance, British propaganda (officially referred to as information services), although relatively cheap and highly successful, has been chronically suffering from the lack of adequate and assured finance. It remains decentralized and is conducted by the Central Office of Information, by the Overseas Services of the B.B.C., and also by the British Council.

Among the varied instruments of propaganda, short-wave radio is by far the most important since broadcasts can reach audiences anywhere in the world and cannot be effectively blocked. Hence much of the money spent on propaganda goes into radio transmitters and programmes and, in Communist states, also into transmitters which jam foreign broadcasts. While this interference is not fully successful, governments can much more easily prevent the distribution of propaganda materials in printed form and have full control over personal travel.

In all propaganda activities the first problem is how to reach physically the people at whom it is directed; it is largely technological and its successful solution depends on sufficient resources and skill. When the target can be reached, there arise difficult psychological problems which are similar to those in commercial advertising: how to capture the attention of the people and how to achieve the desired response. These determine the method of presentation.

A simple way to conduct propaganda is to present news and information as objectively and factually as possible and to leave the listener or reader to reach his own conclusions. A straight-out information service can be politically effective, especially when it reaches totalitarian societies which try to limit their citizens to sources of information suitably vetted by the government. It has the great advantage of attracting attention since the listeners or readers will be generally interested in correcting the distorted and suspect picture presented at home. Complete objectivity is, of course, scarcely realizable and, even in the most factual and dispassionate services, a selection from the various items competing for attention is generally made to emphasize favourable rather than disparaging news. The B.B.C. has earned a justified reputation for concern with truth during the Second World War and since and, in order to retain the interest and the trust of its listeners, it must constantly guard against deviating too far from its high standards of objectivity. Nevertheless, in presenting news to overseas listeners, the B.B.C. could scarcely be expected to stress the backwardness of the British steel industry as much as the up-to-date character of electronics or aviation, or the relative inadequacy of old-age pensions rather than the more advanced nature of the National Health Service.

The opposite technique is that of the 'Big Lie'. It was effectively used by Hitler who acted according to his argument developed in *Mein Kampf*, that a lie, provided it is sufficiently big and is frequently repeated, will be at least partly believed by the masses; most people lack the imagination to conceive that, although repeated, statements are not all true. The censorship of alternative sources of information is essential for this technique to be effective. Falsehood on a minor scale is much less useful and can undermine trust in the sources of information. Hence the United States calls its information activities since the Second World War a 'strategy of truth' and, without quite achieving it, tries to earn the reputation of objectivity enjoyed by the B.B.C.

The form of the news must be reasonably attractive in order to gain attention. The public are not interested in ponderous analyses of the rights and wrongs of any issue but readily respond to simple slogans, however loosely related to it, provided they contain such emotionally valuable words as peace, aggression, human rights, self-determination, etc. Visual impressions and physical demonstrations add greatly to the influence of propaganda. Nuclear explosions and launchings of satellites now supplement the age-long tradition of military parades and of naval demonstrations. Visits by prominent politicians, leaders and artists, even travel by the man in the street, all play a part in drawing attention to the propagandist state.

Not only attention but also positive response is required, and the propagandist must establish a degree of rapport between himself and the people who are his target by appealing to their own local interests, experiences, and outlook. Hence propagandists tend to stress common characteristics and interests—the Japanese spoke of the 'co-prosperity sphere', the Nazis of the Aryan race, the Russians of the solidarity of the oppressed and under-developed countries, the Chinese of the Asians and the 'true' revolutionaries. Where such solidarity is not effectively established, propaganda fails, as shown by the futility of American appeals to anti-Communist sentiments which are not fully shared by others. The influence of propaganda greatly increases through its frequency and consistency over a long period of time and also through the elimination or obstruction of competing sources of information.

Economic instruments

Economic instruments differ from diplomacy and propaganda in that they are not necessarily directly operated by governments. Indeed, in the nineteenth century, international trade which was dominated by the City of London gave the appearance of being divorced from politics and completely autonomous although, as E. H. Carr has forcibly pointed out in *The Twenty Years' Crisis*, this illusion was due only to Britain's unchallenged naval supremacy. In the twentieth century, the close connection between international politics and economics has been re-established. Private interests are still paramount in the international trade of Western Powers, but clearly under a degree of governmental direction. In Communist and also in some new, under-developed countries, trade is conducted by governmental or government-controlled agencies.

The other characteristic peculiar to economic instruments is their great advance towards internationalization. As soon as the governments had assumed substantial economic powers, they began to yield some of them to international institutions. Western trade is circumscribed by the provisions of the General Agreement on Trade and Tariffs (G.A.T.T.), manipulation of exchange rates of national currencies by the membership of the International Fund; members of the European Economic Community and of its Eastern counterpart, the C.M.E.A., have surrendered some of their economic sovereignty to these organizations. There are two reasons why the economic instruments are being internationalized in advance of others. First, considerable economic advantages are secured. Second, although the close connection between economics and politics is now fully appreciated, the direct and immediate impact of economic internationalization on state sovereignty is considerably less than would be the impact of internationalization of such politically sensitive elements as armaments. For the time being, at least, while the most important economic institutions include only Western states, with rare though significant exceptions, the problems arising from their existence have not been politically grave.

Economic instruments are widely employed both in peace and war; in peacetime international trade and assistance are most important, in wartime and during the cold war various measures of economic warfare are employed.

To some extent all countries must engage in international trade in order to obtain some goods which they cannot produce at home, and to sell others with the proceeds of which they can pay for their imports. Beyond this indispensable minimum, international trade provides the benefits of an international division of labour under which the various goods can be obtained from the most efficient and therefore cheapest producer. Free trade, which was actively pursued by Britain between 1846 and 1932, meant to the British an economically most advantageous world-wide arrangement. To the majority of other countries it meant a perpetuation of a situation in which they had little chance of developing their own industries in open competition with the established, more efficient British exporters. Protective tariffs, the most important instrument for controlling international trade, thus arose mainly for economic reasons—to shelter budding domestic industries from foreign competition. These industries, however, were desired not only for economic welfare but also for general political purposes, as an element of state power. The Great Depression, which began in 1929, brought in its train an enormous increase in protective tariffs and also in other devices to keep out imports, such as quantitative controls (quotas) and currency restrictions.

Apart from this protective role, tariffs serve to secure better terms of trade through reciprocal arrangements but they can be used also for more clearly political purposes, as bargaining weapons in negotiations and as instruments of retaliation. Here the elements of size and of relative importance in the foreign trade of the country concerned are decisive. The main buyers of a country's produce or the main suppliers of its vital imports are obviously influential. The Southern States used their position as the major suppliers of cotton for the Lancashire industry in their endeavour to secure British support during the American Civil War; the Austrians were able to bring Serbia to heel through declining to buy her pigs during the so-called 'Pig War' in 1905; Britain exercised a similar pressure on Ireland through the 'tariff war' of 1932–6; Hitler dominated Eastern Europe in the late thirties by offering the only available large-scale market for its agricultural exports—he enjoyed a position which approached monopoly.

Through a deliberate policy, international trade can be directed toward a group of states to enhance its economy but also to reinforce its political coherence, for instance in the various colonial systems, or in the Communist bloc, and in the European Economic Community today.

The post-war trend towards the liberalization of international trade and the establishment of international economic institutions have greatly reduced the freedom of states to control their trade individually. Within the blocs, individual control was being partly superseded by an institutionalized co-operation while the inter-bloc trade could be more suitably discussed under the heading of economic warfare. The situation changed dramatically in the seventies when a long period of rapid growth of international trade was superseded by a prolonged recession started by the energy crisis in 1973. On the one hand, a strong trend towards protectionism arose in large numbers of market economy countries; on the other, inter-bloc trade significantly grew to meet the complementary needs both of the Western exporters needing markets and of the Communist importers needing access to Western technology—and also of the new states requiring both consumption and capital goods. As will be discussed from the systemic angle in the next chapter, international trade became 'high policy'. Naturally this has confusingly altered its use as an instrument of foreign policy and so far the implications are unclear.

Moreover, in the early seventies the growing scarcity of oil and the use of the 'oil weapon' in 1973 by the Arab exporters against the United States and the Netherlands for what they regarded as excessively pro-Israeli policies, raised the possibility of trade also in other crucial raw materials becoming politicized. The experience with oil was inconclusive. As Iran did not support the policies of the Arabs, the oil weapon had only marginal effects; moreover, despite her leading position not only as the largest exporter of oil but also as the only potential source for large additional quantities of oil in the near future, Saudi Arabia was signally unsuccessful in directing United States' policies against Israel. This could be attributed to Saudi mutual dependence on the West as a market, a venue for the investment of the wealth amassed from oil and a major supporter against Communist subversion, and also to lack of diplomatic experience. It is impossible to predict with any confidence when more propitious conditions will arise for the development of this new instrument of economic policy—in fact whether they will ever arise at all.

For a long time investment in foreign countries was private and for economic purposes. It has continued to be so from the time of the great banking houses of the Fuggers in the sixteenth century, or the Rothschilds after the Napoleonic Wars, to the industrial empires and the great oil companies of our own generation. These investments were not divorced from politics, and the national governments encouraged or discouraged them to suit their political aims, but the usual form of direct governmental intervention is assistance and not investment. In all periods economically weak allies had to be buttressed by military supplies and political loans or grants but, since the last war, grants have surpassed all precedents. By the colossal expenditure of over $20,000 million, especially through the Marshall Plan, the Americans helped to restore the economies and to modernize the armed forces of Western Europe. They were dispensing money for military support and for economic aid also outside Europe and were conspicuously successful in restoring the economy of Japan; the funds are continuing to flow out at a diminishing but still substantial rate. In the mid-fifties the Russians began to offer large-scale economic assistance, and their competition with the Americans became an important feature of the cold war. Sometimes the Superpowers courted the same governments, for instance those in India, in Afghanistan, or in Egypt. More often each supported friendly governments; thus the Americans have been helping the Philippines, South Korea, South Vietnam, and Taiwan, while the Russians have been supporting the Fidel Castro government of Cuba. All the colonial Powers, especially France and Britain, have given considerable assistance to their colonies and ex-colonies. Oil revenues have been the source of extensive aid dispensed by the larger oil exporters, originally for political purposes, especially by Libya, but later, after the raising of the oil prices in 1973, largely for helping the poor importers of oil to pay for their imports.

Even in peacetime the unfriendly purpose of economic policies can justify their classification as economic warfare. Such is the boycott of trade which is usually conducted by the people rather than the government, but which may have governmental support—one example is the Chinese boycott of British and Japanese goods in the inter-war period. Or it may be an action against the currency of another state, as in London in 1923 when the French occupied the Ruhr against the wishes of the British.

A state may resort to 'dumping' in order to dislocate production and the world markets—thus in 1958 the Soviet Union resold, with disruptive results, quantities of Chinese tin at a price less than what they themselves had paid to the Chinese. Economic warfare can take also the form of the closing and opening of markets. In 1960, when the Americans became convinced of the hostility of the Castro Government in Cuba, they gradually brought to a halt the imports of Cuban sugar which had enjoyed a privileged market in their country; as a counter-move in economic warfare, in order to stabilize a regime hostile to the United States, the Communist bloc stepped in and offered new markets for this sugar.

In wartime a belligerent may resort to 'pre-emption' of vital strategic materials from neutrals in order to deny them to the adversary, as the British tried to do in the last War with Spanish copper and Turkish chrome.

The best-established war-measure is naval blockade. Britain has been employing it since the times of Elizabeth I, it played an important part in the Napoleonic and the two World Wars, and is still by no means obsolete. The effectiveness of economic measures gave rise to the idea of 'economic sanctions' which were embodied in the League of Nations Covenant as a promising expedient for curbing aggression without military intervention. The League applied such sanctions only once, against Italy in 1935 for her aggression against Ethiopia. The sanctions failed but probably only because the members were half-hearted in their support. In 1951 the United Nations decided in favour of economic sanctions against Communist China, in 1962 it was moving towards such sanctions against Katanga, and, in 1963, against South Africa. It employed them, again rather ineffectively, against Southern Rhodesia.

The cold war led to many measures which can be called economic warfare. Each bloc tried to deprive its opponent of the supplies of strategically important materials and products. Communist international trade is rigidly controlled, and the Americans were making strenuous but not fully successful attempts to curb Western exports of 'strategic' materials to the Communist bloc. As has been noted, the situation changed in the late seventies when the complementary needs of both sides resulted in a great relaxation of restrictions and a great increase in the flow of trade. Consequently interbloc trade largely stopped being used as an instrument of policy and became governed largely by economic considerations.

Military power and war

In contrast to economics, the military field has been fully monopolized by governments. A few individuals and groups possessed weapons independently of governmental control, but these used to be quite insignificant in international relations unless they managed to stage a successful rebellion. Only in the sixties and seventies did resistance groups rise to the position of significant military factors, as epitomized by the P.L.O. discussed in Chapter 4. Nevertheless, the states are strongly circumscribed by international considerations. A unilateral military strategy would be possible only for a state sufficiently powerful to be able to cope with its rivals by itself, or under a policy of isolationism which, as has been explained, is not feasible in the world today. Whether employing the contemporary expedient of alliances and coalitions, or participating in any scheme of collective security of the future, states are no longer in full control of the military instrument.

This instrument looms large in all considerations of foreign policy and is extremely costly; in all states, including the Superpowers, it swallows up a large slice of the national product. Moreover, technological change and the resulting changes in the structure and the operation of international society raise a host of questions about the usefulness of the instrument, questions which are of such a fundamental nature that some of them cannot yet be adequately formulated, let alone answered.

The problem can be easily grasped both from the global expenditure on armaments which, according to U.N. estimates, rose to some $300,000 million in 1977, and from a glance at the issues of a national defence policy. Thus in Britain the frequent criticisms of defence policy arose from the two connected views that this policy has been excessively costly, to the detriment of pressing social needs, and that it has been ineffective, incapable of securing vital national interests. The second criticism is more fundamental, and opinions about cost obviously depend on the answer it receives. Particularly violent was the argument about the usefulness of nuclear weapons. While the unilateral nuclear disarmers regarded the whole expenditure on the nuclear deterrent as immoral and wasteful, more moderate critics stressed the illusory character of the 'independent deterrent' and the inadequacy of the conventional armaments due partly to the diversion of funds to nuclear weapons, and partly to the inefficiencies resulting from the conservatism of military thinking and from the competition between the three traditional services, the Navy, the Army, and the Air Force.

In the United States, concentration upon nuclear weapons in the late forties has given way to a parallel effort in conventional armaments. Although the American economy can sustain both and massive aid to allies, too, the questions of the future size of the defence effort and of its adequacy for ensuring the defence of the country are continuously debated. In France expenditure on nuclear weapons was planned to be steeply rising in the eighties while the effectiveness of conventional arms is likely to be discussed. In the Soviet Union and China where standards of living are low, the competition between guns and butter is stark.

In order to tackle rationally the involved problem of the military instrument, we must clarify its actual role in international relations. Many of the criticisms of military expenditure somewhat naïvely assume that such expenditure, if more efficiently managed, could ensure national security and major national interests. This assumption is untenable. We should not exaggerate the value of the military instrument; complete security is unthinkable in the nuclear era and other, non-military instruments are growing in importance, especially in dealings with the uncommitted countries.

Another source of confusion arises from the fear of another total war and from the resulting attempts to eliminate violence from international relations altogether. Weapons can be used in two capacities—in attack, in order to secure a change, or defensively, to deter a possible attacker and repel him if an attack actually takes place. The policy of nuclear deterrence is not a complete innovation, but merely a modern adaptation of the old Latin adage *si vis pacem para bellum*. The Second World War was a catastrophic disappointment to the naïve disarmers and supporters of disarmament and international organization who believed that violence could be eliminated from the world without an adequate supervisory military force. Nevertheless, although the central role played by the military instrument is now more generally appreciated, the situation is still often obscured by unrealistically sharp distinctions between the states of war and peace and between nuclear and conventional weapons.

As has been repeatedly stressed, state interaction combines both antagonism and community of interests. This means that conflict is never fully separated from co-operation nor co-operation from conflict. Indeed, different periods of history combine the two in varying measures, and the difference between the states of peace and war lies merely in the degree to which one of these elements predominates. If negotiations are the general way in which international issues are tackled and if force is employed only marginally, we speak about peace; if violence is openly employed as the main method of settling such issues, we speak of war. This state of affairs was not altered when the Peace Treaty of Westphalia established peace as the normal mode of international relations in Europe or when international lawyers developed two separate bodies of rules of international law known as the law of peace and the law of war. The cold war, the name commonly given to the immediate post-war period, makes clear how unreal the distinction is. The cold war was neither peace nor war; hostile relations predominated, but not to the exclusion of negotiations, and the use of violence remained circumscribed. We cannot fully explain the place of the military instrument in the cold war either in terms of peace or of war.

Despite our natural preoccupation with the prevention of war, we must not lose sight of the fact that war has been traditionally filling an important social role in international society. Whenever a state wishes to enforce a rule of law which is in its favour but is disobeyed by another state, or to alter an adverse rule, in the absence of any superior authority to deal with these matters, it must unfortunately be ready to resort to violence. It is difficult, if at all possible, to deprive the states of their ultimate right to wage war unless some other effective method of enforcement of law and of peaceful change is devised. Otherwise the world would be frozen without the possibility of change to conform with justice and with changing social conditions, and even existing rights could be violated with impunity. It is arguable that the General Assembly already acts as an agent of peaceful change, although only in a limited fashion. It was instrumental in hastening colonial emancipation but is still helpless even against not particularly powerful members who frequently refuse to comply.

The other unrealistically sharp distinction is that made between conventional and nuclear, or more broadly speaking, nonconventional weapons. The former are less destructive and better understood; their use could be left unlimited or slightly circumscribed by international law without endangering the continuation of the national states or of international order as these exist today. The latter have enormous destructive potentialities, the political implications of which cannot as yet be clearly perceived, and hence their control or, if possible, elimination is the only satisfying solution. In fact, the distinction is much less clear. The devastating Second World War was fought with conventional weapons alone; some of the 'non-conventional' weapons, such as low-yield tactical nuclear devices or mild forms of nerve-gas which only temporarily disable human beings exposed to them, are less destructive than the most powerful conventional weapons. The dangers of 'escalation'—a milder form of warfare gradually leading to more severe forms—are such that a rigid dividing-line is untenable.

The military instrument provides the background of assuredness and stability for diplomacy. 'Negotiation from strength' is a sound precept; without the backing of military power, no state can avoid concessions detrimental to its vital interests if irresistible pressures and threats are brought to bear upon it. The Western Powers withstood Soviet pressures on their exposed position in Berlin, both during the Berlin Blockade in 1948 and 1949, and again, after November 1958, only because they were militarily strong.

Strength alone is insufficient unless the prospective opponent is aware of it and takes it into account. Hence international relations in most ages, particularly so during the cold war, abound in references to and in demonstrations of strength. Armaments and troop formations are displayed during national day parades; naval demonstrations are staged; troops are mobilized or massed along the frontier or shifted to bases in sensitive places. A show of force is a much easier and cheaper expedient than its actual use and it may sometimes be quite effective. It is possible that the Chinese Communists were eventually forced to conclude the dragging armistice negotiations on Korea only by the dispatch of American nuclear weapons to Okinawa, a show of strength implying that they might be used if necessary.

Finally, the military instrument may be actually employed. It is here that the notion of the dichotomy between war and peace constitutes a serious obstacle to understanding because the use of violence is by no means limited to war. Even the classical international law of peace permits the employment of violence which falls short of war under such names as reprisals, measures tinged with a hostile character, or pre-belligerent measures, or measures short of war.

An actual example may explain the distinction made here, and it is best chosen from relations between unfriendly countries in which the military instrument is much more prominent than in the relations between countries which are friendly. Since the Arab countries are hostile, to a very large extent Israel relies on the military instruments. She came into existence through the use of violence, as the result of the victory of the Jewish military forces in the war against the Arabs in 1947. She still relies upon this instrument for her survival, being faced, as she is, with the desire of some Arabs to terminate her independent existence. In order to remind their neighbours of their military strength, the Israelis often parade it and occasionally use it in frontier raids (which serve also the narrower objective of warning against Arab infringements of the border). In 1956, when faced with growing danger from the Egyptians who were receiving military supplies from the Communist bloc, the Israelis used their forces for a large-scale military operation in the Sinai Peninsula. They scored a victory over the Egyptian forces and greatly damaged Egyptian morale but were forced to withdraw under pressure from the United Nations. Then the Israeli military instrument reverted to its previous deterrent role and was actively used only in minor frontier skirmishes, but in situations similar to 1956, it was again used fully in the lightning 'Six-Days War' of 1967, and the Yom Kippur War of 1972; in 1978 it was used for large-scale military intervention in Southern Lebanon to contain Palestine guerrillas and to support the Lebanese Christians.

It is important to note the fact that only conventional weapons have been actually used since 1945, and invariably in a somewhat restricted form. The Americans and the Russians have refrained from a direct clash and, in all conflicts, at least on one side, fighting was done by proxy. The situation shows gradations from guerrilla warfare, sometimes conducted by extremely small groups, as in 1961 and 1962 in Laos, to such approximations to a major war as the conflict fought out in Korea in 1950–51 and in Vietnam in the late sixties. Armed forces were also used extensively outside the context of the cold war, particularly in numerous colonial struggles.

In the policy of deterrence nuclear weapons have served only as a general background for diplomacy and have not been actually employed. The fundamental principle of this complex policy is simple. The weapons are produced and deployed not in order to strike but in order to inspire the opponent with the conviction that they would be automatically employed following any serious attack by him. As long as this policy is successful, the nuclear weapons will not actually be used. Since deterrence is rightly considered as fundamentally important, both sides resort to frequent reminders and demonstrations of their nuclear power; the launchings of satellites and nuclear tests serve these, as well as purely technological ends. Moreover, the Americans, at least, have been devoting much thought to making their deterrent credible, to ensuring that the Russians would be in no doubt as to whether the weapons would be used, if necessary.

It may be added that there is little justification for equating the existence of nuclear weapons with the danger of an all-out nuclear war. Admittedly, the ingenious American doctrine of 'graduated deterrence', based upon the possibility of nuclear conflicts limited in scope, does not sound very convincing. The argument runs that, even if nuclear weapons were employed in any future conflict, neither side would be likely to resort to an all-out attack on the opponent's cities, which would provoke immediate retaliation; hence a war would be fought by small-scale, tactical nuclear weapons alone, or be limited to an attack on the opponent's 'counterforce'. Such limitations are not very credible, however, owing to the dangers of escalation; the side suffering a disadvantage at any level would be sorely tempted to escalate in order to recoup its fortunes, until an all-out war is eventually reached.

Deterrence, or the nuclear balance of power, provides a basis for a certain degree of stability of the present international order, and we have not as yet found any possible substitute. The basis of stability is, however, brittle. It may be destroyed by the proliferation of nuclear weapons or by a technological break-through, e.g. in anti-submarine warfare or in anti-ballistic missiles and by a consequent armaments race. Moreover, deterrence serves mainly conservative aims, to preserve the *status quo*. It does restrict practical revisionist policies by eliminating the likelihood of an immediate all-out nuclear war which would be pernicious to all but, if the limited struggles do not succeed, escalation may eventually lead to it.

So far, war and the use of force have been discussed only as techniques of foreign policy. Their place in international relations can be more fully explained only within the context of the international order.

8 The international system

The nature of the international system

The argument now shifts from the micro-level, the activities of the states and non-state actors, to the macro-level, that of the international system. At the outset this term must be defined.

In the broadest sense, a political system denotes a collection of independent political entities which interact with considerable frequency and according to regularized processes. The term is now increasingly used instead of the partly overlapping traditional terms of 'family of nations', 'international society' or 'community', and several others. It has the advantage of taking us away from the political rhetoric with which the older terms are laden and of enabling us to think systematically, by employing the concept of analytically distinguishable variables evolved in the general systems theory and applied to many other social affairs, e.g. social or economic 'systems'.

International systems lack the two prerequisites of domestic political systems—the social basis of a community and the political structure of a government. Instead of an unconditional agreement on co-operation, on the precedence of some basic common good over sub-group or individual interests, international systems can build only upon a limited and conditional co-operation which sometimes degenerates into complete anarchy. They completely lack a hierarchically arranged government which determines the jurisdiction of all the social sub-groups and has the means to enforce its norms of law. The meaning of sovereignty is quite different in both contexts. While internal sovereignty means that the government is supreme within the political system of the state, that the whole takes precedence over the parts, external sovereignty means that the governments are supreme within the international system, that the parts take precedence over the whole. In other words, while within the states political systems are strongly centralized, international systems are strongly decentralized; in modern terminology, the international system is 'sub-system dominated'.

Nevertheless, as the very terminology employed indicates, international systems do not entirely lack structure and sets of norms which regulate the behaviour of their members, although these structures are invariably much looser and the sets of norms much weaker than those distinguishable within states. These are discussed in the next chapter. The interplay among the units, and between them and the international order as a whole, is affected by the nature of each historical system. Hence an analysis of the nature of the system operating at a given time and place is essential for the understanding of international relations taking place within it. The study of the behaviour of single states, or of states in mutual interaction, is insufficient in itself. From the point of view of the states and other international actors, the international system is no more than the external environment within which they act, offering both challenges to which they have to react and opportunities which they like to exploit. From the systemic point of view, however, the system can often be greater than the sum of its parts. It not only embraces the uncoordinated though interrelated activities of the actors but, in the process, it develops characteristics and a momentum of its own which can lead to unplanned and often very undesirable international events—arms races and wars are the most prominent of these.

Owing mainly to two connected phenomena—the rapidly growing interdependence and the crisis of the territorial state—the internal dynamics of the international system have now greatly increased, extending to a host of economic and ecological problems which cannot be effectively tackled at the state level. Hence the issues of international politics and of the international system in general have been attracting increasingly more attention, both of the statesmen and of the scholars. Many, perhaps most of the latter think in terms of some form of 'systems analysis' and limit themselves to the present and the very recent past. Their thinking should not, however, be divorced from its historical matrix as often they either unknowingly use the frequently inapplicable and misleading insights of their predecessors or they ignore them, at the cost of a great intellectual loss. The modern European tradition of thought about the international system can be broadly divided into three major streams—first, the realist or Machiavellian school, concerned with conflict and power; second, the rationalist or Grotian school, stressing rationality and co-operation; third, the revolutionary or Kantian school, stressing the solidarity of mankind and tending to look at the international system as 'the commonwealth of man'. In the twentieth century intellectual interest in the international system has quickened. One can distinguish four broad phases: major contributions came first from international lawyers and then historians, behaviourists, and, finally, systems analysts.

Conceiving international society as a system and its major components, the states, as well as non-state actors, as sub-systems, conceptualizes reality in a sensible manner. If one begins at the traditional starting-point, that the international system consists primarily of power relationships between nation-states, one extends the analysis both horizontally and vertically: horizontally, by replacing the notion of states as units by that of 'national groups' and recognizing the existence within them of subnational systems; vertically, by extending the network of international relationships beyond power to other issue-areas, notably economic, ecological, and psychological. Thus we end by differentiating a multitude of concrete systems—national, international, extranational, subnational, transnational. Some thinkers, endeavouring to balance the excessive concentration upon states in the past, tend to shift the emphasis to the transnational activities of non-state actors and to arrive at a simplified model of the modern international system as one of a web of world politics in which state activities are becoming increasingly less important and state boundaries mere discontinuities in many fields of human endeavour. This is largely normative, wishful thinking. The multidimensional model proposed here is a much more realistic representation of international reality at the time of writing and the web of world politics model is unlikely to become more useful in this century, if ever.

If, as the systems analysts do, we assume that, along with their historical differences, all international systems show also a certain degree of similarity—they call it sometimes 'cross-systemic isomorphism'—we can fruitfully discuss 'ideal types' of international systems. Thus, for instance, allowing for the fact that most systems fall somewhere in-between, we can distinguish two extreme types: one which is completely dominated by the units and the other by the central institutions of the system. It is also possible to concentrate on historical international systems, particularly modern ones. We shall try to combine both approaches. While it is obviously important to study the balance of power system which was operating from 1648 to 1914, since it has been the basis of the contemporary international society and the source of much of our terminology, it would be difficult, if at all possible, to specify the causes for its disintegration and to estimate the significance of subsequent changes without some theoretical appraisal. By necessity we must break up the chronological flow of events into tidy units, periodize and systematize, and it is preferable that we undertake this operation consciously, explicitly stating the underlying theory.

Analytical categories

Clearly, thinking about the contemporary international system as a whole, in all its complexity, is bound to confront us with great difficulties, especially as the categories employed have been largely developed in the context of its much simpler predecessors. In the first instance, we must take account of the *extensity* of the system which can be analytically broken down into two clear-cut components—(geographical) *scope*, and (functional) *domain*—and the *intensity* of interaction which can be measured by various indices of social communication of which international trade is one of the most important. In all these three dimensions the contemporary system shows considerable advances on its predecessors and therefore its analysis should take as full an account as possible of the degree and nature of these advances and of their implications.

Second, it is useful to distinguish in the international system the elements of 'structure' and of 'process'. By *structure* we mean the characteristic relationships among the actors across time, such as the main types of association and basic types of interaction, whereas *process* refers to forms and modes of interaction, distinguished from structure both by their short time-scale and by their analytic properties.

Third, a category recurrent in all analyses is that of *stability* and *change*. From the systemic viewpoint, 'stability' may be defined as a probability that the system will retain its principal features; that most if not all of its members will survive; that no one state will attain dominance; that adaptation to change will take place without a major war. Of course all social systems constantly change, adapting to changing circumstances. All attempts to make them adapt according to a fixed plan—an ideology—seem to lead to coercion and ossification; this has been clearly demonstrated in the recurrent issue of bureaucratization which has been dominating all Communist systems, despite the great differences in their national variants. Hence blueprints to ensure the stability of the international system cannot be expected to show much promise.

The stability of the international system is often associated with the fourth dimension, the *concentration of power*. There is a fairly general agreement that dominance by one state is undesirable but strong disagreement about what type of system is more conducive to stability: bipolar or multipolar. During the cold war, scholars showed a general tendency to believe that a bipolar system was the less stable one as it is less flexible and as it results in the two antagonists giving each other 'critical attention'. However, despite the largely bipolar structure of the international system, the cold war gradually changed into a detente. Therefore the opposite conclusion seemed to carry more weight—that the concentration upon one another of the protagonists has the positive results of each giving full attention to the other one, and that many of the complexities of a multipolar system are reduced—notably the issues of responsibility are clearer and peripheral conflicts do not as readily spread and escalate. Thus, recent historical evidence seems to indicate that, despite its prominent place as a structural characteristic, the issue of bipolarity/multipolarity is not a decisive determinant of stability. Perhaps the most promising explanatory variable is found in the propensity to risk-taking. On this basis it is plausible to hypothesize that the contemporary international system is stabler than its predecessors because this propensity among the Superpowers is very much reduced owing to the fears of a nuclear war.

Thus, although this is rooted in the traditional state-centric approach which is no longer fully applicable, seeking categories relevant to the issue of avoiding a major war seems to retain a degree of validity and we may continue to seek the criteria for periodization in a combination of three interrelated elements for which Professor Stanley Hoffmann has suggested the name *stakes of conflict*. First, there is the fundamental question of the identity of the units, a question the importance of which can be seen in the transition from the Roman Empire to the medieval system, or from the nineteenth-century system of multinational and colonial empires to the multiplicity of independent states in the present. Then, there is the question of technology, a fundamental change in which, like the invention of gunpowder or of nuclear energy, completely alters the scope of possible actions. Finally, there is the question of what the units want to do to one another, whether they are prepared to co-operate within the existing order or whether some of them attempt to revise it. Attitudes to the existing order are conditioned by the environment, both international and domestic, but influence this order in turn. It is impossible to determine to what extent changes in human ideas, attitudes and desires are the cause or the effect of changed circumstances. Undoubtedly there is a certain amount of circularity; a fundamental change in any of these elements is likely to lead to a fundamental change in others.

A distinction should be made between stable international systems in which the three elements fluctuate only moderately, and others in which changes are so violent that they become revolutionary. The reasons for and the implications of the relative stability of the international system preceding the First World War offer a promising approach to the understanding of the character of the contemporary system.

Incidentally, here we become involved in the perennial argument between the supporters of stability and order against the supporters of revolution and change. This is primarily a normative issue which will be briefly touched upon in the concluding chapter. It requires, however, a mention in connection with the analytical categories because stability—or revolution/change—is often assumed as given. Although it seems impossible to design a fully value-free attitude which would accommodate both, it seems worthwhile to think in terms of *adaptation* of the system, i.e. of change which is acceptable, although not for the same reasons: to the order-oriented politicians because it does not change too much, and to the change-oriented ones because it does not preserve too much.

We can now proceed to a brief outline of the historical international systems which will be discussed largely in terms of the 'stakes of conflict' and of 'extensity' and 'intensity' of the systems. It is a consciously Euro-centric account, not only because the author's viewpoint is inevitably rooted in Western European traditions but also because the Western political system has been the fount and origin of the present global system. Through a complex process of disintegration, followed by expansion and now by a degree of global integration, the Christian Commonwealth of medieval Europe has provided the foundation of the contemporary global system. This is the justification for starting the historical account with the formal ending of the medieval order through the Peace Treaty of Westphalia in 1648.

The balance of power system

The expression 'balance of power' is used to describe a tendency towards an equilibrium which some writers discern in international relations as well as in many social and physical domains; it denotes also state politics aiming at such an equilibrium. Here it is used strictly as a name for the international system between 1648 and 1914. This system lasted over the relatively long period of nearly three centuries and showed remarkable stability in surviving the challenge of the French Revolution and the Napoleonic Wars. Some of the most pertinent questions to be asked are those about the nature of this challenge and the way in which it was met.

There are good reasons for regarding the balance of power as an important innovation in the history of mankind. For the first time since the destruction of the Roman Empire, Europe achieved a fair degree of stability; moreover, it was a stability not of the objectionable hegemonical type based on conquest and domination by a single Power. In conformity with modern ideas and with the forces of nationalism, the new system was plural; it embraced several Great Powers and it gradually transcended the boundaries of Europe. Also, for the first time in the modern period of history, all the participants accepted that the system was important for them. This did not mean that considerations of international order generally prevailed over the selfishness of states, that a community feeling transcending single states became strong. On the contrary, states remained competitive and suspicious, each continuing as the supreme arbiter of its own behaviour ultimately free to break the rules of the system. As in all previous systems, this selfishness could and actually did lead to attempts by states with sufficiently promising power to conquer others and upset the system.

Simultaneously, however, the balance of power was a much more articulated, thought-out system than any of its predecessors. If the member states were not invariably ready to accept the norms it was imposing upon them, they were conscious at least of their common advantage in protecting those norms from being violated by others. When a state made a bid for power, other states tended to join forces in defence; the major challenges of Louis XIV, or Napoleon, or the Kaiser, all eventually ended in defeat at the hands of opposing coalitions.

Stability was based upon the balanced redistribution of territory by the Peace Treaty of Westphalia which established several major states capable of maintaining an equilibrium of power among themselves. Legitimacy was the foundation of the post-Napoleonic settlement and no major changes in units ensued. During the nineteenth century the Ottoman Empire gradually disintegrated, but this Empire had never been essential for the system, and the event was less important in itself than as a harbinger of the disintegration of multinational empires during and after the 1914–18 War. Order was more seriously disturbed when powerful new units arose through the unification of Italy and Germany.

Although all states, large and small, powerful and weak, were participating, theoretically on the basis of sovereign equality, in fact the balance was maintained only by the few powerful states; it was a balance of power among the Great Powers and the system depended on their coexistence. Fortunately there were several such Powers, as five seems to be the minimum number facilitating a steady equilibrium. Two Great Powers would tend to end in a headlong clash or try to carve up the world into two competing spheres of influence; four would tend to form two rigid combinations of two states, each of which could be altered only by an extremely dangerous reversal of alliances. Like triumvirate governments, the balance of power based upon three units would be inherently unstable since a state would have little opportunity for realignment and therefore would have a strong incentive for striking first; the only possible regrouping following a war would be an obviously risky and therefore unlikely combination of the weaker of the victorious Powers with the defeated Power. Thus it was for the benefit of the system that there were so many Great Powers.

Stability was increased by several favourable circumstances. There were no dramatic technological changes like the recent invention of nuclear weapons; there was ample room for economic development; overseas expansion was a useful safety-valve which enabled states to increase power without seriously endangering rivals and offered wide scope in the game of compensations, necessary to maintain balance. Industrialization and colonial expansion were much more promising means of augmenting state-power than the subjugation of another European state. Territorial expansion in Europe was impeded not only by other members of the system who were apprehensive that the equilibrium might be destroyed but also by communications, which remained very poor until the end of the nineteenth century, and by the growing influence of nationalism—Bismarck would have found it very difficult to occupy France for any length of time after the Prussian victories in 1870–1.

The system was based on the continuation of the traditional pursuit of security by each state through its own efforts, but it offered opportunities for negotiations instead of fighting and for the conclusion of temporary alliances to counterbalance the power of others. When challenges to the equilibrium could not be staved off in a peaceful way, wars did break out, but they were not fought to eliminate the opponent. Restraint in victory was not due to altruistic reasons but to a realistic concern with the system, to preserve the vanquished state as a potential future ally.

Domestic pressures became less cogent. Religion lost its fanatical appeal, mercantilism and absolutism gradually weakened within the Great Powers. The rulers and diplomats of all countries were conscious of their 'corporate identity' and agreed upon the legitimacy of the balance. Hence they found no reason to interfere with powerful and growing transnational links, the intellectual links based on the Enlightenment, and the commercial links of international trade. Tolerance at home and abroad extended to the domestic systems of other states. Since full flexibility of the balance of power demanded that states should be completely independent, the lawyers perfected the theories of state sovereignty, of impenetrability of territory, and of non-intervention.

Only the more powerful states were necessary for the maintenance of the system but the theories of sovereignty were extended to lesser Powers, too, first in Europe, then in Latin America, and subsequently throughout the world. These smaller states were admitted on the basis of 'sovereign equality', but their role in the system was mainly passive. They were not so much potential allies who could make an impact on the power of the alliances as potential areas of expansion for a Great Power which could, through conquering them, become dominant. Though in themselves the smaller states were not essential for the working of the system, their elimination presented problems too difficult to be worthwhile. Within the framework of flexible alliances, the Great Powers could not agree upon any workable division of Europe and they usually preferred to make use of the much more profitable and politically less dangerous opportunities for expansion outside Europe. Only one smaller state was divided, and the experience was scarcely encouraging: Russia, Prussia, and Austria carved up Poland rather gingerly in three consecutive partitions towards the end of the eighteenth century, but the Polish question remained one of the most explosive topics of international politics. The incorporation of dissatisfied Poles who occasionally rose in arms scarcely enhanced the power of the occupants. They managed to maintain an equilibrium in Eastern Europe but probably could have done so more efficiently had Poland been left independent.

The system was severely challenged by the French Revolution. In the first place, the Revolution introduced changes at home, with a new regime which assumed full and intolerant governmental control over the citizens and prepared the path for Napoleon with his exorbitant ambitions. Internationally, the Revolution destroyed the solidarity of a homogeneous Europe through its ideas, and the balance of power through its military victories; as the result of the Napoleonic Wars all frontiers became unstable and Europe was rent by ideological and national antagonisms of a fundamental nature. The victors decided in favour of legitimacy, of the restoration of the pre-war system in preference to the accommodation of the new forces. The balance was restored and so was France as one of its essential units, under her previous Bourbon rulers and within her pre-revolutionary boundaries.

Between 1815 and 1914 the system evolved the Concert of Europe. Britain rejected the Russian proposal for the much further-reaching Holy Alliance, a loose world government to be worked jointly by the Great Powers, with the right to intervene in the domestic affairs of other states. The Concert was merely a loose consultative institution which refrained from intervention in the domestic affairs of states. It permitted many small wars, but prevented these from becoming general and thus upsetting the balance of power. Nineteenth-century Europe thus neatly balanced conservation and change and can be credited with many positive achievements. The behaviour of the Great Powers was, on the whole, moderate, as epitomized in the lenient peace concluded by Bismarck with Austria after her crushing defeat at Sadowa. There was general stability and no states disappeared, but such major political changes as the emancipation of the Balkan people from Ottoman rule and the neutralization of Switzerland, Belgium, and Luxembourg were achieved with little violence, international law developed and, towards the end of the century, colonial expansion came under a degree of internationally agreed regulation. It must, however, be borne in mind that these achievements cannot be credited to the balance of power and the Concert of Europe alone since they were made possible by exceptionally favourable conditions for the economic and political expansion of the system.

In the latter part of the century these conditions began to deteriorate, as did also the attitude of Germany, one of the five Great Powers. The process of colonial expansion ground itself to a halt when there were no further lands available for occupation, and economic expansion degenerated into competition among rival national economies; in contrast to his last great lenience to Austria, which had been defeated only four years earlier, Bismarck severed Alsace-Lorraine from France after the 1870–1 War. This led to a continuing French grievance and deprived the international system of a large proportion of its flexibility: from 1871 France was permanently aligned against Germany. Instead of working through fluctuating alliances, the system broke up into two opposing camps; slowly but gradually the diplomatic fronts hardened and eventually clashed in August 1914.

This account, concerned with power relationships, has already covered the issue of the expanding geographical scope of the international system. The functional domain equally expanded—the powers of the ideas of the French Revolution had a widespread impact, international trade, functional links across national boundaries and travel all grew apace, the first international institutions were established, all leading to a greatly increased intensity of interaction. Although all these trends were cumulative, they were not fully incorporated into the analyses of the international system, both contemporary and retrospective. Partly this was due to the tendency of the governments, especially those of the dominant Power, Great Britain, to divorce them from power politics, and partly owing to the difficulties of conceptualization. These two difficulties were to persist in the subsequent inter-war period. Despite the fact that, in contrast to the nineteenth century, economic problems assumed a central importance especially as the result of the Great Depression, they still did not become issues of high policy like the issues of territorial and ideological clashes.

Search for a new order

Being the only known modern form of international order, 'balance of power' dominated the political thought and activities in the first half of the twentieth century. Attitudes to it varied. Some thinkers considered it as the only possible promise of peace, others rejected it as having been ultimately responsible for the First World War. Whether endeavouring to improve the working of the existing system or to replace it by something new, they were all thinking in terms of the nineteenth-century experience and were employing the concepts inherited from it.

The system gradually changed from a European to a global one. Around the beginning of the century, two non-European states, the United States and Japan, were admitted to the status of Great Powers but, as their participation did not become as intimate as that of the European states, the system thus became looser. At the same time, through her naval challenge to Britain, Germany made a bid for the extension of the balance of power system from Europe to the oceans of the world. She confidently but vainly expected that, provided there was a sufficiently powerful German navy to form the nucleus of a naval coalition counterbalancing the British navy, other naval Powers would rally against Britain to establish an equilibrium in naval power similar to the balance of power in Europe. However, the distrust of Germany's power and intentions was such that, instead of pursuing the balance of power formula and joining the weaker side, the two great naval outsiders, the United States and Japan, preferred to align themselves with Britain.

With sporadic intervention by the United States, the Concert of Europe managed to settle several acute crises early in the century, but it gradually lost all remnants of its flexibility. In vain did Sir Edward Grey try to galvanize it into another effort in 1914. It finally came to an end with the outbreak of war in August.

The First World War was a traumatic experience for mankind. Having been lulled into a feeling of false security, people found it difficult to adjust themselves to a long war, unexampled in its scope of destruction, and to contemplate the possibility of its recurrence. To many, the war meant complete bankruptcy of the old system and a challenge requiring a completely new response. They sought this reponse in a much more tightly organized new type of international order. The states kept their positions in it; indeed, the League of Nations Covenant guaranteed the perpetuation of their territorial integrity and political independence, while the principle of national self-determination gave them a powerful moral and ideological justification. They retained also the ultimate right to resort to war in pursuit of national ends but the League of Nations introduced a collective security system which was to replace the insecurity of fluctuating national alliances.

The inter-war world was profoundly disturbed. All the three elements determining whether a system is stable or revolutionary, pointed towards revolution. First of all, the composition of international society changed. Two Great Powers, defeated Germany and communized Russia, were temporarily out of the game, many new states had come into being, and Europe ceased to be the exclusive centre of world politics. With the advent of the totalitarian ideologies, first Communism, then Fascism, and finally Nazism, international society became extremely heterogeneous and some of its members intolerant and proselytizing. Second, the technological changes, the development of the aeroplane, the tank, the radio, provided new instruments for expansive policies in peace and in war. Third, the totalitarian regimes determinedly set out to use these instruments and pursue such policies.

The horrors of the First World War failed to persuade the people of all or even the majority of states that their interest in peace demanded a world order which must take precedence over their traditional national interests. The collective security system was ineffective because the Great Powers, both within and outside the League, were insufficiently determined in their support for it. Indeed, in terms of power politics, it proved pernicious. It utterly destroyed the possibility of flexible arrangements and it reduced the likelihood of action against an expanding nation. This was due to the simple fact that the states directly interested and hence ready to act had to persuade and carry all those less directly concerned. The inter-war period witnessed an uneasy and inconclusive struggle between the new idea of collective security and the traditional one of the balance of power. From the very inception France tried to revive the latter, first by seeking a guarantee from the United States and Britain, then through a ring of alliances, the *cordon sanitaire* around the defeated *Reich*, then through the Locarno Agreements with Germany which ambiguously attempted to reconcile balance of power considerations with the collective security system, and finally by seeking an alliance with the Soviet Union.

The geographical scope of the international system had encompassed all the accessible parts of the globe already in the nineteenth century and only the frozen wastes of Antarctica were further added in the inter-war period. The domain of the international system increased with the establishment of the League of Nations and the International Labour Organization (I.L.O.). Nevertheless, when economic issues disturbed the world, as the gold standard in the early twenties and much more acutely, the Great Depression from 1929 onwards, despite some ineffective *ad hoc* efforts to seek an international solution, they were dealt with by individual states, at the cost of severe economic setbacks and widespread unemployment. In retrospect, the need for some effective form of international co-ordination of individual national policies became so obvious that it laid the foundation for a wide extension of the domain of the international system in the post-war period. Simultaneously, the rapid advance in the technologies of transport and communications provided the means for a great increase in the intensity of international interaction.

When they looked back upon the failure of the League to prevent another war, the adherents both of the balance of power and of collective security agreed to one thing—that a stable order in the inter-war period had been precluded by the lack of co-operation among the Great Powers, notably the recurrent differences between the French and the British, the isolationism of the United States, the long exclusion from international society of Germany and Russia, and the lack of co-operation between the Western Powers and Russia in the late thirties. Franklin Roosevelt at first envisaged a world order founded upon the idea of the Great Powers policing their spheres of influence, a system of loose world government which de Gaulle called permanent intervention. This did not appeal to the outsiders and anyway became impossible owing to the differences between the Soviet Union and the Western Powers. Nevertheless, the idea of a Concert among the Great Powers served as the basis for the United Nations which attempted to establish a collective security force supplied mainly by these Powers and permitted regional security sub-systems. The collective security system did not materialize and only the latter survived. Even before the end of the war institutions were established to co-ordinate the important domain of international economics. In 1944 at Bretton Woods there were established the International Monetary Fund (I.M.F.) and the World Bank; talks were started for the establishment of an International Trade Organization which was not, however, destined fully to materialize.

Attempts to establish a new stable international order failed for the fundamental reason that the Great Powers that really mattered were reduced to the two Superpowers—the United States and the Soviet Union. Germany and Japan, the two defeated states, were temporarily eliminated; China was still very weak and France had not yet recovered from defeat; Britain was economically exhausted and it did not take many years to show that she could no longer rank as one of the 'Big Three'. Independently of the fundamental ideological differences, disagreement between the two Superpowers was partly the consequence of their number; neither balance of power of the nineteenth-century type nor collective security could possibly work with only two protagonists.

The bipolar system and its evolution post-war

By the criteria previously suggested, the post-war system was highly revolutionary. Its composition was rapidly changing—the Superpowers were new to their status and responsibilities, the other Great Powers to their loss of status, the rapidly multiplying Asian and African states to their independence. The nuclear weapons and the ballistic missiles were new and terrifying instruments of destruction. Both Superpowers were governed by ideologies which rendered them intolerant in international relations: the expansive ambitions of Communism were confronted by determined American opposition.

Until 1947 it was not clear that the world was becoming bipolar. It did not seem likely that the United States, unravaged by war and the only possessor of nuclear weapons, could be effectively challenged by the Soviet Union for some time at least. The antagonism between the Russians and the West soon deepened, but at first it was Britain, and not the United States, which was the main opponent. It seemed likely that the Americans might withdraw into their traditional isolationism, as the Russians undoubtedly hoped they would. The Americans, however, took over the lead when the British were incapable of bearing the financial strain of continuing to play their world role: in rapid succession there came a British request for financial aid, an agreement to merge the British and the American occupation zones in Germany, a withdrawal of British aid to Turkey and Greece. The watershed was the Truman Doctrine of March 1947, in which the President announced that the United States would take over British responsibilities in Greece and Turkey and that it would assist any country willing to resist Communism. The cold war was joined.

Without attempting to apportion the blame for starting the cold war, it may be regarded as a sparring match between the two giant states, a succession of moves and of countermoves. The process of involvement was gradual. The acute conflict between the United

States and the Soviet Union was at first confined to Europe but gradually spread to other continents—first Asia, then the Middle East, and finally also Latin America and Africa.

With a speed surprising to the West, the Russians developed nuclear weapons. Eventually, the Soviet Union and the United States were not only threatening each other with nuclear extinction but were confronting each other everywhere; any change, in whatever part of the world, could affect the delicate equilibrium between them. This balance of power was quite different from the nineteenth-century one which had been based on the inter-play among five Great Powers, every one of which had an interest in the survival of the others. Neither the Americans nor the Russians had a real interest in each other's survival since each would have found the world safer without the other. Apart from mutual fear, no powerful external restraints existed to prevent them from destroying each other. Admittedly, during the brief period of its nuclear monopoly, the United States did not act on the advice of the few extremist though logical advocates of a preventive war against the Soviet Union but simply used this monopoly to counter-balance Soviet preponderance in other, conventional weapons. Then the Russians developed their own nuclear weapons and the struggle resolved into the uneasy equilibrium of deterrence. In non-nuclear matters the balance remained precariously delicate since a light swing in favour of either side could sway the scales, perhaps irretrievably.

The United Nations' idea of a Concert of the five Permanent Members of the Security Council was hopelessly out of date. The United Nations continued negotiations on collective security, disarmament, and some other aspects of international order, although with rapidly decreasing prospects of success, but the emerging international order was clearly bipolar. In the cold war, states were inevitably attracted to one of the gravitational poles, either through the pressures of one Superpower or through fear of the other. The Soviet Union consolidated a ring of Communist regimes around her Western frontiers and the United States successfully counteracted this move by supporting economically and militarily Western European states and by forming the NATO alliance. Since the NATO formula worked reasonably well in Europe, the Americans used it in other regions, supplying aid, establishing bases, concluding alliances. Two supranational blocs seemed to be gradually emerging, the world was being sharply split into a Communist part and what the Americans call 'the free world'.

For a short while the trend seemed more or less inexorable. There was no place for neutrals in the bipolar world and both the Russians and the Americans regarded such states as India with suspicion; both applied the maxim that he who is not with us is against us. The bipolar character of the post-war world was revealed so suddenly that many people were blinded to other aspects of reality and became convinced that eventually the whole world would become divided into two antagonistic blocs facing each other—that the bipolar system would become increasingly tight. The prospects seemed poor, both for mankind faced with the danger of an atomic holocaust, and for the individual national states which seemed to be increasingly at the mercy of the Super-powers. The Soviet Union organized her empire rigidly and main-tained sufficient troops in and near her 'satellites' to ensure compliance; the Americans used subtler pressures, but their series of alliances amounted to no less than a counter-empire, less hierar-chical but nevertheless clearly centring around the United States.

Then the forces of nationalism successfully asserted themselves. Instead of becoming tightly bipolar, the international order began to take a different direction. By the late forties consolidation within either bloc had not made much progress. Attempts to establish a 'Third Force' in Western Europe proved abortive but in 1948 Yugoslavia successfully defied the Soviet Union. The Soviet-Yugoslav dispute was misleadingly clad in an ideological garb but was in fact fundamentally an assertion of national ambitions against Soviet tutelage. Although this was not clear at the time, the dispute indicated that, after all, the Russians would not be able to fully consolidate their empire, and that consequently there was no prospect that such an empire and its American counterpart would swallow up the whole world.

Also the world outside the two opposing blocs refused to be moulded into tight bipolarity. Particularly important was the stand adopted by India. With the background of their traditional tolerance, their abhorrence of polarities and of militarism, the Indians chose to stay out of the two rival blocs. They, with the

Yugoslavs, offered a pattern of behaviour for other emerging states in Asia and later also in Africa, which preferred to remain non-committed. Gradually it became clear that one-third of mankind had decided against joining the two rival blocs, that a large portion of the globe would remain non-aligned.

In the fifties, also, the two opposing blocs loosened. Western European Powers, with a restored economy and revived spirit, were unwilling slavishly to follow American policies. In 1956 Britain and France engaged in their abortive Suez expedition; de Gaulle's challenge to United States' leadership plunged NATO into a prolonged crisis. The nationalist riots in Hungary and Poland were a clear warning to the Russians that their 'satellites' could not be subdued and exploited indefinitely and led to some loosening and liberalizing of the Eastern bloc. In Poland the process was halted but, in 1966, Rumania began to pursue an individual foreign policy, rejecting Soviet direction, and, in 1968, the Czechs liberalized their domestic regime, eventually provoking the Russians into a large-scale military intervention. Perhaps most importantly, the Sino-Soviet rift which came into the open in 1958, gradually developed into an acute conflict, and eventually, from the early seventies, China gradually began to restore relations with the United States. Although China developed nuclear weapons, her conventional armies deteriorated and she became preoccupied with domestic political troubles—the prolonged Cultural Revolution in the late sixties and the struggle for Mao's succession in the late seventies. Moreover, she did not manage to secure international following and thus her potential as a third World Power temporarily dwindled.

Nor did the two Superpowers retain their nuclear monopoly. Britain, France, and China have produced operational nuclear weapons and a number of further states have acquired sufficient nuclear technology, whether for peaceful or military uses, to be able to produce such weapons. Although the existing and, even more so, the potential weapons could not possibly equal those of the United States and the Soviet Union and would not be likely to affect the balance of nuclear power between the two, they endow their owners with much greater independence and flexibility in their foreign policies.

Even in the late seventies the outlines of the emerging new

international system were still dim and fluctuating. It was possible to discern the three blocs established in the fifties and sixties—Western, Communist, and non-aligned, the latter very much looser than the other two—but it may be better to call the system 'polycentric' since the centres of power are many and include not only blocs but also single states and the United Nations. Apparently the national states are not going to lose their importance. Not only the two Superpowers but other, less powerful states are playing a significant part in international relations. When it comes to purely regional issues, the weak African states working in concert successfully prevail against either Superpower. They have adopted the General Assembly as their favourite forum and the United Nations has become a spokesman on their behalf. The future of the nuclear weapons is confused. While deterrence continues to keep nuclear danger at bay, it remains uncertain whether further states will acquire nuclear weapons and unclear what the implications would be. The Nuclear Non-Proliferation Treaty (N.P.T.) which came into force in 1970, although strongly supported by the Superpowers, does not seem to offer much hope.

The historical pattern of the balance of power thus cannot be adapted to modern realities, while the blueprints for collective security seem unrealistic. An additional reason for uncertainty is the dramatic growth in both the extensity and the intensity of the international system which further complicates the task of dealing with the traditional issues of international peace and security. First of all, the geographical scope has drastically extended through the growth of the technological means for the exploitation of the oceans and for the use of outer space for communications and, at least potentially, also for military purposes. Second, the functional domain of the international system has extended in many functional areas and the number of international institutions has multiplied. Finally, the intensity of international activities has grown, not only within their new scope and domain but also within the traditional ones. It was impossible even to conceptualize, let alone to actually accommodate, all these changes into a traditional model of an international system. The new post-war international order is still at an early stage of its making and the elements already visible may completely change. All we can do at the moment is to try to identify some of the main problems it is facing.

Needless to say even this task can be performed only tentatively. Blinkered as we are by past experiences and by present problems, we may fail to identify what is going to be important in the future. The problems of today, pressing as they are and important as they are likely to remain in the near future, may be superseded within a few years by new problems, without necessarily having been fully resolved. This was clear in the late seventies about the central problems of the immediate post-war period—the cold war and anti-colonialism—to which now the disturbance of the international trading and financial systems and the issues of resources, especially oil, have been added. These will be briefly surveyed in Chapter 10.

9 Instruments and agencies of international society

International society and its members

It has been repeatedly stressed that international systems are more than the mechanical sums of interaction among their members, that they exhibit a certain structure and develop sets of norms for state behaviour. We shall now discuss how the historically evolved institutions of the contemporary international system cope with the issues confronting us.

International society does not include many units—only in the second half of the twentieth century did the states surpass 150 and other organizations become distinct international actors. Like many organizations with few members, international society has not developed many specialized organs and instruments; in fact, until recently nearly all the activities carried out on its behalf were undertaken by the Great Powers. However, harmony of interests between international society and the members acting on its behalf cannot be assumed to exist in all situations. As has been argued, states act primarily in order to secure their individual national advantage and it is hard to imagine that they would ever refrain from pursuing it. Indeed, if we look into the operation of the Concert of Europe, we readily perceive how complex is the connection between individual and social roles; sometimes the suspicion arises that the presumably social role serves as a mere disguise for the pursuit of purely selfish interests.

While we recognize the confusion and hypocrisy implicit in the situation, we must bear in mind that international order fully depends upon the co-operation of the Great Powers and cannot possibly work if the vital interests of any of these Powers are adversely affected. Practical difficulties do arise and have to be solved in each single case. In theory the conundrum can be explained fairly easily. On the one hand actions against the vital interests of one's state cannot be in the interest of the system to which the state belongs, since the system would automatically become not worthwhile; on the other, once the preservation of international order in general is accepted as a vital national interest, the state may have to go quite far in overriding its more selfish interests and values.

Over the last hundred years, but mainly since the last War, there have arisen numerous agencies and institutions working for international society as a whole. They act simultaneously also for their individual state-members and occasionally in the interests of a group of them or even of a single Power alone, but their major function is to act on behalf of international society. The new institutions express the evolution and sophistication of international politics just as division of labour and specialization express them in economics.

The operation of the post-war international system is not only complicated by the rise of non-state actors but is continuing to share the difficulties of all organizations consisting of a small number of members which apply to its most important units—the states. Theoretically, all states interact on the footing of sovereign equality, as if they were similar in most significant respects. In fact, they differ not only in power but also in their political systems and institutions, in the ideologies they profess, in the attitudes they adopt to the international order. They are pronouncedly individualistic and must be realistically accepted as being so. Failing large numbers, it is impossible to impose any far-reaching codes of behaviour which would rigidly apply to all, or to arrive at any significant statistical rules according to which such behaviour could be predicted. In a domestic society which numbers millions of individuals, norms of behaviour do not lose their general validity if they are occasionally infringed by a few; it is even possible to predict the frequency of such infringements. In international relations any statistical prediction of the probability of behaviour of units which are so different in some vital respects, would be very unreliable; moreover, violation of the norm by one single state may deprive it of its significance. What, for instance, would be the value of outlawing war or nuclear or any other weapons of mass-destruction if one Great Power refused to submit? The Superpowers and often also other Powers can be compared with the mighty feudal barons who could not be expected to accept all general norms of behaviour; not statistical forecasts but an analysis of their individual policies and attitudes is required for most purposes.

Hence, while it is possible to analyse an issue in a domestic society in the abstract, without going into the identity of the parties, such analysis does not take us far in international relations. The identity of the state involved is as important as what is at stake. It is, for instance, clear that the Irish claim to Ulster creates an issue of quite a different nature than would a Soviet claim to a part of Finnish territory. An objection to a trivial infringement of diplomatic etiquette by one of the Superpowers can create an issue very much graver than the Albanian claim to the southern part of Yugoslavia. Weaker states have always found it difficult to deal with those more powerful. They have often been forced to seek the protection of greater Powers, arriving at a position of dependence similar to that of vassals in the feudal system; sometimes they were eventually absorbed by these Powers. Otherwise they formed combinations, like the Swiss or the American Federations, which reduced their inequality in relation to the more powerful states. Discrepancies have greatly increased today because the accumulation of power by the two Superpowers can scarcely be matched while, under the aegis of the United Nations, new states have been coming into existence which could never have reached independence in the harsher climate of the pre-United Nations world.

Through their oscillations between periods of stability and revolution, over the last few centuries the relations between international society and its members have greatly increased both in scope and intensity. In every period of change they have to be rearranged, and the more ramified and intensive they are, the more difficult does the task become. The problems of our own generation are considerably more involved than those following the French Revolution, not only because they are graver in themselves, but also because we have to deal with them in a much more complex framework.

Until now international societies have been subservient to their members, although depending on the type of structure, not always to the same degree. On the whole, since the War the two Superpowers could influence international order and were less subordinate to it than the several Great Powers participating in the balance of power in the nineteenth century. If, however, as seems likely, international society continues its evolution towards polycentrism, its structure and the operation of its agencies will logically become more autonomous, and this seems to be happening already.

Norms regulating the behaviour of states

A society cannot operate without some normative social control of the behaviour of its members. When every member is a law unto himself, anarchy prevails, behaviour is unpredictable, and no social order can be maintained. International society differs from national societies in that it consists of states instead of individuals and is only loosely organized. Nevertheless, analogies from a society of individuals are not unwarranted, provided they are not pushed too far and the differences are kept in mind.

A legal system is the most highly evolved form of expressing social order; but human behaviour is governed also by many other, non-legal norms, those of morality and of what is often called *mores*, such as custom, etiquette, or fashion. Some thinkers prefer to derive the highest of these norms, those of law and morality, from higher superhuman principles, but it is possible to explain them, together with the other norms, as a mere expression of social needs. Societies differ in the degree to which they permit variety in human behaviour and in the stress they put upon conformity. On the whole, the nature of the rules is governed by their social importance and is expressed in the type of sanction provided in cases of breach. If the social importance of the rules is slight, mild social disapproval suffices. For instance, a woman waiving the dictates of fashion may be slightly ridiculed or hampered in her social intercourse with more fashion-conscious individuals. If the dignity of an institution or occasion calls for the wearing of customary attire, anyone not so dressed may be refused admission—thus a woman in a sleeveless dress may not be allowed into an Italian church.

Social sanctions increase with the degree to which human behaviour seriously affects others. Some norms are incorporated in the law of the country and are enforced by central authority which tries to prevent their infringement and punishes their violation; law cannot, however, meet the whole range of socially undesirable possibilities, and is therefore supplemented by the rules of morality which are not enforced in the same way but are generally considered to be quite important. The sanctions for the violation of moral rules lie not only in individual conscience (which is assiduously trained in the desirable direction at home, at school, and in all social intercourse) but also in strong social pressures. If cruelty to children is to be avoided, law can define only a limited number of punishable offences, but a person treating children cruelly, although not committing any of these offences, is likely, if discovered, to be condemned by his friends and neighbours. This too is a strong form of sanction.

These well-known and rather simple distinctions are mentioned here because they illuminate the more abstruse nature of the norms regulating the behaviour of states. As in domestic societies, the scope and nature of international norms are determined by those of social needs, but there is an important difference in the degree of social agreement which can be reached about them. By definition, domestic societies embody a considerable measure of fundamental social consensus, without which they would not have come into being or would disintegrate. If such social consensus existed internationally, it would lead directly to world government. International order is based not so much on the consensus of its participants as on the physical fact that states coexist and cannot escape from interaction. It is a world characterized mainly by the stark necessities of a Hobbesian society which has not yet evolved a fully articulated social contract.

Interaction among states is much less varied than interaction among individuals, and therefore the customs and conventions, the *mores*, of international society are not quite as complex and voluminous as those among individuals. As in a domestic society, the sanction for their infringement is social disapproval of suitable severity. In stable periods, such as much of the fairly homogeneous balance of power system, the customs were generally accepted and observed; in revolutionary periods, however, they are deliberately and flagrantly violated. A good illustration may be found in the determination shown by the Bolshevik rulers of Russia, after they had come to power, to substitute direct relations with the people of other countries, and later with their Communist parties, for traditional diplomatic relations. In a few years, when the dust had somewhat settled, the Russians reverted to the traditional forms of diplomacy, including ceremonial dress and titles, although they did not abandon their attempts at subversion.

One source of the norms of international behaviour is found in history, in the way in which states, especially the Great Powers, have actually been behaving. Hence the great importance of precedent. International relations abound in situations in which states seem to be governed less by the merits of the specific case than by the fear that they would establish an unwelcome precedent. For instance, it seemed very likely that the adamant Soviet refusal to consider the Japanese claim for the return of four small islands of the South Kurils after the Second World War was not mainly due to the strategic and fisheries interests involved; the Russians were determined to avoid a precedent for allowing the Chinese to press for the revision of the 'unequal' Amur Treaty which had established the Sino-Soviet boundaries in Siberia in the nineteenth century.

Further-reaching is the concept of 'legitimacy' which denotes some form of international recognition of certain norms of behaviour. This can be based on a bilateral relationship alone—e.g. the leaders of both Superpowers occasionally refer to the 'rules of the detente', meaning the norms of mutual behaviour arising from their past behaviour and understandings, though the substance of these is admittedly often disputed. Legitimacy can be conveyed by decisions of international organizations, not only the United Nations, but also regional ones. Thus the United States was helped by the Organization of American States in confirming the legitimacy of its 'quarantine' declared in the crisis arising over the Soviet missiles on Cuba in 1962, while the Organization for African Unity was the decisive legitimizing agency for the Cuban military interventions in Africa in the late seventies.

Legitimacy is increasingly more achieved by what is sometimes termed 'organized persuasion', international debates about what the norms should be, in which individual states become so strongly aware of the views of others and of the repercussions of their behaviour that they can be persuaded, sometimes more or less coerced, to accept rules which they do not readily find acceptable. When the cost of opposing the opinion of other states becomes prohibitive, it becomes rational to adopt the prudential policy of adaptation, of abandoning or attenuating the pursuit of national interests, however much cherished. An outstanding example is the way in which Western Powers gradually accepted the powers of the General Assembly to deal with the issue of apartheid in South Africa which they justifiably considered as being of essentially domestic jurisdiction and hence not within the competence of the U.N. Another example referred to in the next chapter is the British acceptance of an extended Exclusive Economic Zone contravening the principle of the open seas cherished by the British. The General Assembly, being the 'town meeting' of the world, acts as a central source of organized persuasion on the world-wide scale. It is of particular importance in a world rent by ideological, racial, cultural, and economic conflicts which render accommodation difficult. In a lesser geographical or functional scope, the same process goes on in all international organizations. The total result is of a fundamental importance to the functioning of the international system: from being essentially self-centred in the past, states have now inescapably become what some sociologists call 'other-oriented'. Needless to say, this does not mean that they necessarily yield to the desires and susceptibilities of others but they are forced to take them into account and assess the cost of overriding them.

Justice and international morality

When public debates over the justification of national policies arise internationally, invariably some resort is made to the principles and ideals of justice and of international morality. Each is referred to under a variety of terms and meanings, all of which boil down to one basic consideration—a justification which is internationally acceptable.

It is extremely difficult for us to conceive of principles which are universally acceptable, first, because decision-makers remain bound by the priorities they have to accord to their respective national interests and, second, because it is operationally difficult to conceive of a world community within which we could apply such principles on an equal footing, without giving priority to one's own nation and special obligations. The problem can be readily demonstrated by the obstacles besetting the practical application of the now generally accepted principle that rich states have some form of obligation to help those which are very poor. The degree of sacrifice and the nature of the incentives greatly vary. In the late forties, the Americans found it easy to spend about two per cent of their G.N.P. on the Marshall Plan, not only because their economy was buoyant but also because they found the expenditure well worthwhile owing both to what they perceived as urgent security reasons and to the high chances of success. At the end of the seventies, when faced with the issue of accepting as members three relatively poor Mediterranean countries, the existing members of the E.E.C. were hesitant about a similarly generous policy—the decision-making machinery, involving the consent of all the nine members, the relatively lower security benefits likely to accrue, and possibly also greater doubts about the likely efficacy of large-scale aid, all played a part. On a world-wide scale the United Nations has not come anywhere near the achievement of its proclaimed principle that the rich countries should devote at least one per cent of the G.N.P. to aid. Underlying the hesitations in all these cases, apart from the Marshall Plan, are the justified doubts about the efficacy of aid: striving towards economic equalization at the international level cannot be reasonably conceived as a purely distributive policy—aid flowing from the rich to the poor—but must perforce involve the improvement of the domestic performance of the recipients over which the donors have insufficient influence.

What makes the notion of international morality so ambiguous is that its meaning has never been clearly defined nor has there been agreement concerning the relation between the norms of individual and international morality. One school of thinkers, following Machiavelli, deny the existence of international morality altogether; others, like Kant, equate international morality with private morality; most thinkers accept the existence of international morality but differentiate between it and individual morality.

A realistic analysis of international relations cannot accept at their face value the repeated protestations of statesmen of all countries that they are governed by moral rules. Clearly morality is often invoked under various names merely to provide a respectable garb for the pursuit of selfish state interests. It is a convenient common justification for claims which run counter to somebody else's legal rights. Since law is conservative and allows no claims in equity or way for revision, those demanding revision invariably invoke morality. The Versailles Peace Treaty was a binding legal agreement, but the Germans represented it as an immoral dictate of the victorious Powers determined to oppress them; it is similarly possible to question many legally established boundaries on the basis of national self-determination.

Nevertheless, it does not follow that Machiavelli was correct in rejecting the existence of international morality. Despite the lack of agreement as to its extent, international morality cannot be adapted to selfish ends in all circumstances. In our generation a claim for the revision of frontiers for the purpose of uniting a nation can be advanced and accepted as being morally justified, but, if made on grounds of strategic or economic necessity, such a claim would receive little sympathy from other states and from international public opinion so that no statesman would think of advancing it. This is the first important reason why moral norms must be accepted as an influence upon the behaviour of states: this behaviour is perceived and evaluated in moral terms. Even if, in order to pursue a vital national interest, states sometimes ignore or flout international public opinion, they are generally interested in finding favour with it.

Second, the demarcation lines between domestic and international affairs and between states and individuals are not quite as sharp as they used to be. In the nineteenth century states alone had a standing in international law, and their treatment of individuals, provided these were their own subjects, was their own domestic affair. The excesses of Nazism have led to the extension of some rules of individual morality to the treatment of individuals by states. Human rights are now covered by a number of norms of behaviour some of which have hardened into law although most of them are limited to declarations and belong to the realm of morality. However, the Final Acts of the Helsinki Conference of 1975 have renewed the early post-war interest in human rights and have provided the basis for important subsequent international disputes about their application to the Soviet Union.

Also the moral sentiments of statesmen as individuals must be remembered. It is safe to assume that, at least when their national interests are not seriously affected, they usually prefer to act in a way they consider moral rather than otherwise. This is particularly true about the practice of the United Kingdom and the United States. In the exceptional security these countries had enjoyed in the nineteenth century, they had the opportunity of thinking in moral terms and not, as continental statesmen usually did, in terms of necessity, of the *raison d'État*. There is, however, some substance to Dr. Reinhold Niebuhr's contention that, far from extending their moral rules to international politics, men tend to use these politics as an outlet for their immoral propensities—that they are moral men living in an immoral society.

The extreme Kantian proposition that international moral norms are identical with those governing individuals belongs to the realm of the 'ought'. Everything ultimately should be reduced to the measure of man, but this does not alter the fact that states are not individuals and that the individuals acting on their behalf consider first their national advantage. Morality constitutes only a vague corrective to their behaviour, perhaps most concretely by providing advanced standards for the interpretation and evolution of international law. Beyond that, a vague obligation to respect some basic human rights and to meet the urgent needs of individuals, even if they belong to another state, may be on the way to becoming a generally accepted norm of international morality; in the case of large-scale natural calamities, when the national government has insufficient means for coping with the distress, other states which can afford it are expected to help, and a similar sense of responsibility for assisting the poorest countries is gradually growing.

International law

Just as the most important norms governing the behaviour of individuals are embodied in domestic, or as the lawyers call it, 'municipal' law, so some norms governing the behaviour of states are embodied in international law. Even so, the identity of name does not indicate an identity of nature. International law operates in quite a different social context, without the foundations of an overwhelming social consensus and of a central authority which endows its rules with sanction. States differ from individuals in that they are not subject to law; international law is not a law above states but one between them. This is a situation so anomal-

ous for a legal system that some professional lawyers used to deny
the legal character of international law altogether, claiming that it
lacks the distinctive characteristic of effective sanctions. Sovereign
states and an international legal system of the same type as domestic legal systems are logically incompatible: either the states are
truly sovereign and recognize no superior, in which case there can
be no legal rules binding them; or, if such rules exist, then states are
not truly sovereign. The contradiction is resolved by the theory of
consent which claims that the binding character of international
legal norms is founded upon their acceptance by states, explicit or
implied. Thus being bound by international law becomes a form of
exercising sovereignty. In the classical definition of sovereignty in
the Wimbledon case, the World Court emphatically declined 'to
see in the conclusion of any Treaty by which a State undertakes to
perform or refrain from performing a particular act an abandonment of sovereignty'.

Since international law is based upon such an uneasy compromise, it is not surprising that the evaluation of its significance
ranges so widely. Some regard it as a sham, while others claim
that, if only given a chance by politicians, lawyers could draft a
comprehensive code which would ensure peace upon earth.
Neither view does full justice to the true nature of international law
which tries to reconcile the contradictions inherent in the coexistence of sovereign states and international order and is the expression both of state-sovereignty and of its limitations.

International law is universal: its norms apply to all states,
independently of their power, status, geographical position, ideology, and so on. Variations, however, appear in the relations within
certain groups of states. Some variations are regional, for example,
already those in the last century in Latin America and, since the War,
in Africa, the Middle East and, in a particularly pronounced form,
in Western Europe. Others are according to membership of milit-
ary/ideological blocs, the membership of NATO or the Warsaw
Pact. Finally, a dual system of norms has been developing along
the North/South axis in favour of the new, developing states. The
customary standards governing both international and domestic
behaviour have never been applied to them with full rigour; furthermore, by the seventies, as part of the nascent New International
Economic Order, a dual system of rules was emerging, imposing

on the developing states some rights without corresponding obligations.

A sociological analysis of the norms of international law shows that they fall within three categories. First, there is what Professor Georg Schwarzenberger calls the law of power. It consists of the rules helping to maintain the political framework, the existing hierarchies based upon power. Here belong norms ensuring the independence of states and non-interference in their domestic affairs, peace treaties, boundary agreements, alliances, etc. Then there is the law of reciprocity which regulates areas less vital for power-purposes where the states are willing to accommodate the interests of other states in order to obtain reciprocal benefits. This is the most numerous group of international norms, which covers many fields, for instance, diplomatic immunities and extradition, trade and communications, or limitations of warfare. Finally, there is an international community law, still at a rudimentary stage; examples of it can be found in the regulation of the slave trade, or of international rivers, or in the standards of economic good neighbourliness in the General Agreement on Trade and Tariffs.[1]

Like all normative systems, international law incorporates certain principles of natural law but a historical survey of its development shows that it has been formed more through state practice than through logical deduction from such principles. It is intimately linked with the balance of power system within which law performed the important task of laying down the rights and duties of states in relation to one another; most of its basic rules were developed in the fifteenth and sixteenth centuries when the system was coming into being.

International society is fully decentralized and possesses no legislature, but nevertheless it incorporates such a fundamental rule as *pacta sunt servanda* which enables states to develop the law through numerous reciprocal treaties. Some arrangements and clauses recur in the treaties regulating a given subject-matter and often serve as a basis for international customary law; this simply means that after a time they are taken for granted and need not be

[1] Georg Schwarzenberger, *Power Politics*, 3rd edition, Stevens & Sons, London, 1964.

explicitly written into new treaties.

Another important consequence of the decentralization of international society is the absence of a central executive authority which could enforce the law. This, however, does not matter overmuch because this law does not attempt the unenforceable—it does not impose upon states rules liable to infringe their vital interests. States retain the ultimate right to use force and resort to war, and preserve an exclusive jurisdiction over domestic matters; despite some attempts to do so, intervention was never established as a legal institution. Although breaches of legal rules do not entail penal consequences, they are rare. Social pressures within international society usually provide a sufficient sanction since all states wish to have the reputation of being law-abiding, which makes treaties with them more respected and desirable and, to some extent at least, shelters them from blackmail and hard bargaining to which less principled states can be subjected.

Within the balance of power system, international law was quite adequate and, with the partial break during the French Revolution and the Napoleonic Wars, it gradually developed into a fairly comprehensive system of rules. The general moderation and acceptance of the system made workable the law of power, despite its rudimentary nature; against the background of security, reciprocal interests gave rise to a rapid development of treaties, especially regarding commerce, while numerous conferences and a few permanent institutions began to extend the law of community.

When the balance of power system began to decline in the twentieth century, the many efforts to spread the 'rule of law'—to develop international courts, to extend international law to the prohibition of the use of force—were bound to fail. Law is an expression of social order and is only marginally a formative element within it. The main reason why these attempts failed was that the reformers confused the law of power with other groups of norms. The laws of reciprocity and community could develop and prosper only against the background of the security ensured by the operation of the balance of power. When this security disappeared and the law of power had to be fitted to a new international system, any attempts to extend community norms to the field of power were extremely naïve. Moreover, the legal system which had a

European and Christian basis required adjustments to accommodate non-European and non-Christian states.

Since 1945 international law has lost much of its traditional meaning. The basic distinctions between domestic and international matters have disappeared and those between private and public acts have become blurred; many rules concerning territorial jurisdiction or the law of war and neutrality have been violated to the point of nullifying them; the new problems of nuclear weapons, outer space, the exploitation of the sea-bed, or propaganda, cannot be readily solved. The conflicts in the bipolar world were so sharp that no security could be found within it; the relations between the two hostile blocs were so unsettled that the law of power could not provide a reasonable background for reciprocity and co-operation, and in fact neither reached its previous level. Simultaneously, the interaction within the blocs became so intimate that in some respects it superseded traditional international patterns and began to resemble interaction within integrated political societies.

The sharp dichotomy of the bipolar world may now be resolving into a new polycentric order and, instead of becoming sharply differentiated into intra- and inter-bloc relations, international law is reverting to its more general function. However, it would be unrealistic to expect a return to the norms of the golden age of international law based upon the balance of power. There has been no break in the continuity of international law, as it is easier to adapt old concepts and institutions than to build up from scratch, but obviously the law of the new order will have to be a new kind of law. Much of it will be conceived to satisfy the functional needs of international society as a whole rather than to deal with security and power and will therefore fall within the hitherto rudimentary category of rules of 'community law', sometimes called also 'new international law'. So much has been done in this domain since the last War that, following Professor Myres McDougal, some international lawyers suggest that we should regard the making of international law as a form of international decision-making, differing from the political one only in that it employs legal or quasi-legal forms.

A good example of this process is found in the evolution of the law of the sea, arising primarily from the development of technologies which made possible the exploitation of the sea-bed for minerals and led to serious over-fishing and depletion of the most popular and accessible species of fish. New norms were arrived at in many ways. The earliest post-war measures were established through unilateral national declarations which were then repeated by other nations, sometimes fairly readily, like the extension of exclusive national rights to the continental shelf by the United States, sometimes with a long delay, like some Latin American claims to exclusive fisheries rights over a 200-mile zone. International conferences of the major states involved were periodically convened to ensure the conservation of whales and of fish stocks in the North Sea, without much effect.

The most important instrumentality in the development of the law of the sea and one which offers most promise for other important issue-areas likely to arise in the future, proved to be a series of general U.N. conferences on the law of the sea (U.N.C.L.O.S.). Two of these were held in the late fifties and codified the law, especially that dealing with the delimitation of the continental shelf. It also came close to an agreement on the width of territorial waters over which states hold exclusive jurisdiction, the width of which has been historically developed, varying as much as between three and twelve miles. A series of sessions of a new conference were convened in the seventies, demonstrating the expedient of collective persuasion as a method of international law-making. Debates were prolonged, the deadlines were never met, and the ultimate solutions arrived at can be regarded as only a minimal programme, not anywhere near solutions optimal for the international community because they greatly extended the jurisdiction of the individual states over what used to be the open seas, the common heritage of mankind. At the same time, however, they halted the continuing depletion of fisheries and made sufficient progress towards a legal framework for the exploitation of sea-bed resources to prevent the recurrence of acute international conflicts. Although the conference was unable to reach agreement about a proposed new International Sea-bed Authority to control the exploitation of the sea-bed outside the domain of individual states, it did reach one on the principles of twelve-mile territorial waters and of a 200-mile Exclusive Economic Zone. There is little doubt that a similar procedure would be adopted if and when technological advance makes likely the exploitation of Antarctica, the only unappropriated part of the land masses of the globe.

A large proportion of the new international law is, however, likely to take the form of the law of international institutions.

10 International institutions

Global international institutions

International institutions will be considered here only in their role as agencies of international order. They constitute too specialized and complex a field to allow more than the broadest outline of their historical development, structure, and activities.

People can save themselves much effort in personal life by developing routines to deal with recurring needs and situations. In social behaviour such routines take the form of institutions. In a broad sense the word institution includes such *ad hoc* arrangements as international conferences to settle a specific matter, but generally the name is reserved for establishments which operate continuously. The majority of the existing well over 2,000 international institutions are non-governmental; they combine national associations and individuals, and many of them represent relatively esoteric interests which have no direct bearing on politics. But even if singly these institutions exercise only a negligible impact on international relations, the thin strands, when woven together, constitute quite a strong rope. They represent so many individuals and organizations with transnational affiliation that they form links among the national states.

Out of the total number, over 200 institutions are intergovernmental, more than half of them regional; they include some which are politically important; only these will be discussed here. The term 'international organization' is used interchangeably.

The first international institution, the Geodetic Union, was established only in 1864, and the subsequent proliferation of others clearly reflects an increased intensity in international relations. This was made possible by the exceptional stability of the balance of power order, but subsequent disturbance of this order did not spell the end of the existing institutions; on the contrary, it led to the establishment of additional ones, including those of greatest political significance, the League of Nations and the United

Nations. History is important in explaining the nature of the institutions. They are not as closely connected with the balance of power as is international law. In fact, they largely represent twentieth-century forces and ideas which came into being after the balance of power system had stopped functioning effectively. Nevertheless, there is a close link between law and institutions. Some of the most important institutions have pronouncedly political objectives and are run by politicians and statesmen, but the drafting of their charters and their interpretation remain in the hands of lawyers. Legality, conformity with the constitution, is a necessary feature of any state policy which intends to win the support of the other members. Legal arguments can stretch interpretation of the constitution to great lengths, but there is a limit even to their flexibility and the other members sit in judgement.

Here we come up against the fundamental difficulty of all international institutions inherent in their dual role which theoretically need not, but actually sometimes does lead to incompatibilities. On the one hand, institutions pursue certain international objectives and work on behalf of international order. On the other, the member-states enter these institutions with the same interests as they had before, and expect them to be satisfied, or at least not infringed. Ideally there is a harmony of interests—co-operation within the institution improves the chances of satisfying the interests of states, thus compensating for incidental inconveniences—but this is not always the case. Britain, for instance, a faithful though perhaps not very enthusiastic member of the United Nations, found if difficult to accept United Nations' actions directly affecting British policies, such as the condemnation of the Suez expedition in 1956, or the violent and often uninformed and unrealistic attacks on British colonial policy.

In order to estimate the dual role of international institutions as instruments both of international order and of the national policies of the members, we should consider their place in the three realms of international politics dealt with by the laws of power, of reciprocity, and of community. As is the case with international law, institutions succeed in direct proportion to their distance from power politics: the less they affect the power-position of states, the more are these states likely to co-operate. Therefore immunities for diplomats were more acceptable than the outlawing of war; since mail is strategically much less important than telegraph and radio, the Universal Postal Union has been more successful than the International Telecommunications Union.

The lines between reciprocity and community cannot be sharply drawn because once reciprocity among states reaches a certain level, it leads to the development of the rudiments of a community; for instance, reciprocal trade agreements have now established the good neighbour principle which has become incorporated in the relevant international institution, the G.A.T.T. International organization has been both the result of certain common objectives and the agent for the development of community ties. Where reciprocity has remained the rule, it serves as a convenient specialized channel for reciprocal arrangements.

Co-ordination and reciprocity were successfully carried over from the nineteenth century and further developed in the twentieth, when many new institutions were added to those few previously existing. The development of institutions concerned with power politics began only at the turn of the century. The two Hague Conferences in 1899 and 1907 unsuccessfully attempted to provide a legal framework intended to limit the use of force and to facilitate the solution of disputes through non-violent means. The conventions concluded did not go very far and the only institution established, the Permanent Court of Arbitration, was not in fact either permanent or a court, but merely a panel of names from which the parties could choose arbitrators for the settlement of any issue they might wish to submit. International institutions concerned with power politics arose only in the wake of the 1914–18 War, as a result of the bankruptcy of the old order based on the balance of power. Although the political relevance of the League of Nations in inter-war politics was not perhaps great, it is well worthwhile to return to the assumptions underlying its establishment, assumptions which illuminate the nature of international organization although they are not widely accepted today.

The League of Nations and the United Nations in historical perspective

The League of Nations was conceived as a comprehensive institution. In President Wilson's words, it was not to be 'merely a league to secure the peace of the world' but also 'a league that can be used for co-operation on any international matter'. The League was born out of the shock caused by the First World War, and its main activities were to maintain peace. Hence its work in pursuing international co-operation on the lines developed in the nineteenth century did not become fully appreciated until its political activities had failed in the mid-thirties. Discussion of the non-political activities can be left to the following section; historical perspective depends mainly on the setting within the international system and the relations among the Great Powers of the period.

The framers of the Covenant of the League of Nations did not agree in their attitudes to the problems of peace. At the one extreme there was President Wilson, whose approach to international relations was evangelical, who wished to achieve through the League what another prominent statesman, General Smuts, called 'an inner transformation of international relations and institutions'. A concert of power was to end entangling alliances which he blamed for the war; a collective security system was to replace power politics. This was not, however, the attitude of the British, who played the next most important part in the establishment of the League; they regarded the League largely as an improved contemporary version of the 'Concert of Europe' which had so well served their national purposes in the nineteenth century. The French were concerned with guarantees against renewed German aggression; hence they were particularly interested in the machinery of sanctions against a covenant-breaker, and their first draft included far-reaching provisions in this direction, including the establishment of a commander-in-chief with a permanent staff. Thus, while Wilson conceived the League as an instrument of international order, the British and the French saw in it mainly a new instrument to serve their respective and differing national interests and tried to mould it accordingly.

During the twenty years of its active existence, the League changed its character several times. When the Americans did not join it, rather unexpectedly, the small neutral states became the spokesmen for collective security and the principles of international order. Their views, however, did not prevail since they were merely 'consumers of security'. The character of the League depended on the views of its Great Power members, those who would have borne the brunt of any collective action.

France and Britain deliberately pursued their respective national interests and therefore did not see eye to eye about the treatment of Germany and the role of the League. At first Germany and the other defeated countries were kept out and the League amounted to a loose association of victors and neutrals to preserve the peace settlements. In the mid-twenties, in conformity with British views, Germany and the other defeated states were admitted in the vain expectation that they would co-operate from the inside in the maintenance of international order. After the danger of Nazism had become clear and Hitler had left the League, the Soviet Union joined it and vainly tried to shape it into a fully-fledged anti-Nazi alliance. For most of its existence the League stubbornly but futilely pursued general discussions about international order which will be analysed in the following section.

In 1945 the victors at least did not fundamentally disagree about the treatment of the defeated enemies. They formed the new international organization, the United Nations, as an association of 'peace-loving' nations directed against the potential aggressors, which in 1945 meant the defeated states. The United Nations was to be tougher and more realistic than its predecessor; the American President and Secretary of State made sure that this time neither the United States nor the Soviet Union would stay out.

The Charter was signed in June 1945 but, before the United Nations even started its operations, it had become obsolete. The new nuclear weapons were first exploded in July and used with telling effect against Japan in August. The preponderance of the two Superpowers and the differences arising between them made unimportant the original agreements on the treatment of the defeated states—and, in any case, both sides soon deviated from their drastic provisions. Until 1947 the United Nations uneasily tried to bring the Charter into operation, working, as envisaged, mainly through the Security Council in which the Superpowers tried to reach agreement, usually in vain.

In its early period the United Nations served, to a large extent, the ends of American national policy. The Russians could paralyse the Security Council by their power of veto, but the Americans made extensive use of the large majorities they could command in the General Assembly and shifted there the centre of political activities. The process culminated in 1950 when the Russians temporarily withdrew from all the organs of the Organization; it is quite possible that they were preparing for a final withdrawal and were grooming a rival Communist organization, the Partisans of Peace. However, when the Americans made use of their absence and secured United Nations' support for their action against the Communist North Koreans who had attacked American-protected South Korea in June 1950, the Russians immediately returned in order to impede further action in the matter and to safeguard themselves against the repetition of such happenings.

Between 1955 and 1957 the composition of the United Nations dramatically changed with the mass admission of Asian and African states. The United States, its European allies and Latin American supporters were no longer in the majority in the General Assembly. The new members were interested not in the cold war but in anti-colonialism; the Soviet Union supported them in accordance with her traditions and secured their reciprocal support or at least neutrality. Since 1958 the United Nations has become increasingly identified with the Afro-Asian bloc and its aspirations.

Anti-colonialism, however, is bound to abate with the rapid emancipation of colonies, and the Afro-Asian members are likely to take an increasing interest in other aspects of the international order. On the whole they are treating both Superpowers with suspicion and are refusing to side with either. They have been repeatedly urging them to refrain from behaviour endangering the peace of the world and to get on with disarmament. The Afro-Asian states are 'consumers of security', as had been the small contingents drawn from themselves and not from the Great Pow-not quite as great. They have, for instance, established the principle that United Nations intervention forces should consist only of contingentsdrawn from themselves and not from the Great Powers. The U.N. force on Cyprus included British troops only because they were available on the island and were indispensable for the constitution of the force. So far international organization has been unable to make much progress towards a new type of international order mainly because its Great Power members could never agree. Although there is no guarantee that the smaller Powers will be capable of agreeing on much beyond their present anti-colonial objectives, it is at least not impossible.

We will turn now to the organization and the activities of the League of Nations and the United Nations which are of more than purely historical interest. The existing traditions may not be perpetuated by a United Nations in which the smaller Powers are preponderant, but they will serve at least as a starting-point.

The structure of global institutions

World-wide international institutions centre round the United Nations with a membership of over 150 states and with a wide competence in security, political, and non-political matters. Loosely co-ordinated and connected are thirteen Specialized Agencies which deal with more limited technical aspects of world co-operation and generally have a somewhat more limited membership. Some of them, such as the Universal Postal and the International Telecommunications Unions (U.P.U. and I.T.U.) date back to pre-United Nations days, but most of them, for example the Food and Agriculture Organization (F.A.O.) or United Nations Educational Scientific and Cultural Organization (UNESCO), or World Health Organization (W.H.O.) have been established towards the end of the last War or since.

The structure of all these institutions is basically similar, although it shows some variations according to how relevant their activities are for power politics and to the role played by the Great Powers. All the members are represented in some form of assembly, in the United Nations itself called the General Assembly. The principles of sovereign equality and of unanimity are sometimes slightly modified; in the International Bank and International Monetary Fund, voting is weighted by the amount of contributions made by the members; and in the General Assembly of the United Nations, recommendations—which have no legally binding force—require only a two-thirds majority even on important matters.

The position of the Great Powers and main contributors is reflected by another body, generally called a council, in which they are assured by the constitution or given in practice seats together with a small number of other members. The relations between the council and the assembly vary from institution to institution, and within them, in different periods, but in no case is the council an executive body acting on behalf of the assembly. The United Nations has three specialized councils—a Security Council of fifteen, with five Great Powers permanently represented (Britain, China, France, the Soviet Union, and the United States); an Economic and Social Council of twenty-seven, without permanent membership, and a Trusteeship Council in which countries administering and not administering trust territories are equally represented.

From the point of view of international order, extremely important organs of the institutions are their secretariats. Whereas the assemblies are based on the principles of sovereign equality of all members, and the councils, however imperfectly, endeavour to give some expression to power gradations, the secretariats act on behalf of the institution as a whole, as distinct from its individual members. Although he commands no state machinery, the Secretary-General of the United Nations is an internationally important personality. He cannot exercise much initiative on behalf of international order since the powerful members can successfully obstruct, but he is responsible for implementing a policy once agreed by the organization and can interpret his instructions with some degree of latitude.

The position of the Secretary-General acting on behalf of the United Nations as a whole, maintaining international order even against the national interest of powerful members or their blocs, is extremely precarious. He represents an organization which has no power or means except those provided by its members. The only tangible element of power which he can wield is international public opinion as expressed by these members. He must be always watchful in estimating what this opinion is and, even with the greatest care, he cannot avoid eventually antagonizing some members. This was the fate of Trygve Lie, the first Secretary-General, who accepted the American view that the Communists had committed aggression in Korea and allowed full United Nations' support for American action. This happened also to his more cautious successor, Dag Hammarskjöld, who pursued an active United Nations' policy in the Congo, thwarting Soviet designs. Khrushchev's contention that no individual can be neutral is justified in the conditions of our generation, but his demand that the position of the Secretary-General should be split into a 'troika', a committee of three representatives of the three blocs (Communist, Western, and non-aligned) would have led to a complete paralysis of the organization. While the bloc would be able to exercise their veto, the Organization could not conceivably do much for international order. Following the successful part played by the Secretary-General in the Cuban missile crisis in 1962, apparently the Russians accepted this.

Both in the League and in the United Nations, members retained their sovereign positions and the immunity of their domestic affairs from interference. However, this immunity in the United Nations was somewhat conditional, limited to matters 'essentially within the domestic jurisdiction' of the members, and the General Assembly gradually eroded it, the majority considering the ensuing disputes to be political rather than legal. Arguing that any domestic affair which affects international peace and security stops being essentially within domestic jurisdiction, the General Assembly has been freely discussing and making recommendations upon colonial matters, human rights, some aspects of the governmental system of the members, all of which would have been considered entirely out of court by the Assembly of the League of Nations. Moreover, by Article 25 of the Charter, the members agreed 'to carry out the decisions of the Security Council in accordance with the present Charter'. This means that, provided the five Permanent Members concur, they, together with an additional four members of the Security Council, could impose far-reaching obligations on other states. The Permanent Members are immune because they can prevent an unacceptable decision by exercising their power of veto.

Maintenance of international peace and security and other activities of comprehensive international institutions

The attempts to ensure the maintenance of international peace and security through suitable institutional means is best explained by a comparison with the maintenance of peace in a domestic society. In 1918, when the Covenant of the League was written, international society was still in an anarchic condition. When negotiations and other methods for settling differences failed, states resorted to force and, in turn, could be restrained only by force or its threat. While in domestic societies the widespread use of violence was ended by a degree of social consensus on the vesting of the monopoly of force in a central authority and by the establishment of such an authority, only very radical thinkers could believe that these were feasible, at least within foreseeable time, in international society. The institutional devices did not go quite so far but were an attempt to adapt some domestic institutions serving the maintenance of peace to the looser structure of international society.

One group of these institutional devices dealt with force. Its use by individual states was strongly circumscribed, or even prohibited; plans for collective security envisaged internationally administered sanctions against a peace-breaker; proposals for disarmament aimed at eliminating the danger of armaments-races and the temptation to resort to war because armaments were abundant. Another group of devices imitated the domestic machinery for negotiations and adjudication of disputes, including the courts of law, and tried also to find some method for a peaceful change of legal relations to correspond with social changes. Finally, since satisfied states are more likely to remain peaceful than dissatisfied ones, various welfare measures, generally desirable for their own sake, were also aiming at peace.

The League of Nations Covenant circumscribed the legality of war. Members were allowed to resort to it only after certain prescribed procedures and 'cooling-off' periods had been adhered to. Moreover, the members expressly undertook to preserve each other's territorial integrity and political independence against external aggression (Art. 10). In the twenties, many international efforts went into 'closing the gaps' in the Covenant and outlawing war altogether. This was ostensibly achieved by the Briand-Kellogg Pact in 1928, which was signed by all states, with only insignificant exceptions. The signatories renounced war as an instrument of national policy and undertook not to seek the solution or settlement of disputes of whatever nature or origin by other than peaceful means. Although at the time this was not generally realized, war nevertheless remained lawful in at least five instances, notably in self-defence. The Charter of the United Nations, the signatories of which undertook to refrain from the use and threat of force in their international relations, explicitly authorized self-defence (Art. 2, para. 4, and Art. 51).

States could scarcely be expected to rely upon agreements alone, and the Covenant of the League therefore provided for collective sanctions against a convenant-breaker (Art. 16). There were to be diplomatic and economic sanctions which would be applied by the members automatically, simultaneously, and comprehensively, and optional military sanctions to be applied at the recommendation of the Council. The Charter introduced centralized sanctions, and did not differentiate between the non-military and the military ones. All sanctions were to be applied on the binding orders of the Security Council which was to have at its disposal a collective security force. Finally, both World Wars ended in the disarmament of the defeated aggressors, and the Covenant provided for a general disarmament or limitation of armaments, while the Charter, having proposed a collective security force, limited itself to a provision for their regulation.

In the light of the historical record, all these attempts to circumscribe the use of force in international relations were unsuccessful. Plans did not materialize, agreements were hedged with escape clauses or interpreted so narrowly that they became meaningless, force was used in many minor conflicts and also on the largest scale in history in the Second World War. The activities of international institutions in this field largely amounted to statements of goals and aspirations. They were not, however, fully devoid of practical effect. Even the most limited form of United Nations' intervention, such as inscribing an issue on an agenda and passing resolutions, is an influence, admittedly not an imperative one, which is taken into account by states contemplating the use of force. The United Nations was unable to stop some outbreaks of violence but effectively confined them and facilitated their termination.

United Nations' 'presence' is now an important international factor in many minor conflicts which do not directly affect one of the Superpowers. Sometimes a group of impartial observers is employed, as the U.N. Commission on India and Pakistan (U.N.C.I.P.); sometimes it is a body of trained military personnel used for supervision, most signally in Palestine (U.N. Truce Supervision Organization, U.N.T.S.O.); finally, it can be a proper military force. The first force of that type was used in the Suez zone to supervise the cease-fire and the withdrawal of the attacking forces (U.N. Emergency Force, U.N.E.F.). It was a brilliant improvisation due largely to the drive of Dag Hammarskjöld who recruited it among the few neutral states who had contingents available. Another, even larger force was used for various tasks in the Congo, including the politically explosive one of preserving the unity of the state. This force was involved in actual fighting and acquitted itself well. U.N. intervention forces are difficult to organize. They have to be recruited from states acceptable to the host country and they are not assured of finance. For a while the very survival of the Organization was threatened because of the debts accumulated for the maintenance of the forces in the Middle East and in the Congo, to which the Soviet Union, France, and some other states refused to contribute. Even so, a small U.N. force facilitated the transition from Dutch to Indonesian rule in West Irian (New Guinea) in 1963, another small force was sent to Yemen in 1964, a larger one to Cyprus, and in 1978 one to the Lebanon.

In the field of pacific settlement of disputes, international institutions not only added conciliation by their organs and judicial settlement by the World Court to the previously existing procedures, but also prodded and encouraged states to resort to pacific settlement instead of fighting. The achievement was, however, largely procedural. Many procedures exist, but resort to them does not ensure that settlement will be achieved. The standards by which international disputes are solved remain vague. The maintenance of peace without qualifications can easily lead to appeasement, to the satisfaction of aggressively-minded states at the cost of the weaker ones. 'Justice' is mentioned several times in the Charter but is insufficiently articulated to provide a suitable criterion.

The trouble is that most disputes are not legal, not about the respective rights and duties of the parties, but political, aiming at the alteration of such rights and duties. Both the League and the United Nations were established in the aftermath of World Wars primarily to maintain the *status quo*, the settlements arising from these wars. Both had only extremely vague provisions for procedures to be employed in revision of treaties and in peaceful change. The main 'peaceful change' (meaning one not involving a major war) in the inter-war period was the revision of the Peace Treaty of Versailles which took place outside the League. By contrast, the

United Nations has partaken in much of the change since 1945, notably in accelerating progress towards colonial emancipation. Pressures by the United Nations have occasionally been great enough to force states to abandon their legal rights and to agree to change but, needless to say, the influence of international organization both in the processes of conciliation and of peaceful change depends, to a very large extent, on the power of the parties; by and large the Superpowers are very much harder to persuade than smaller Powers. No states, however weak, yield on really vital interests, e.g. South Africa on apartheid.

The preamble of the Charter states the determination of its members 'to promote social progress and better standards of life in larger freedom' and for this end 'to employ international machinery for the promotion of economic and social advancement of all people'. This so-called 'functional co-operation' includes three distinct objectives. First of all, international co-operation in technical matters which had been dealt with by international bureaux already in the previous century has been maintained and extended to other fields, for instance, civil aviation and peaceful uses of atomic energy. Second, as a reaction against the excesses of totalitarianism and against the sufferings caused by the last War, humanitarian influences have found expression in many attempts to secure internationally the observance of human rights and the achievement of higher standards of social welfare. Third, since legitimate grievances could cause wars, economic and social progress could provide an additional way of preventing them.

When considered from each of these three angles, the record of international functional co-operation looks different. Technical co-operation has further advanced, e.g. in economic or cultural matters, or regarding outer space, but scarcely in accordance with the growing needs of international interaction; where power considerations and selfish national interest are affected, progress has been painfully slow. The humanitarian influence has undoubtedly been established as part of international life. The very acceptance of the fact that the human rights of anybody, anywhere, are an international concern, and that the whole of international society is, at least to some vague extent, responsible for the economic and social welfare and progress of all its members, constitutes an important departure from the pre-war state of affairs.

Somewhat dubious is the assumption that the elimination of economic and social grievances is likely to help in the prevention of war. It would be more convincing if conceivably such grievances could be fully eliminated. In fact, they can only be alleviated. There is no need for cynicism, for the humanitarian justification of international activities in this field is in itself sufficient, but it is rather illogical to assume that the hungry who are given half a loaf will become more peaceful. On the contrary, not being fully preoccupied with their struggle for existence and having more energy, they may become even more turbulent.

With its nearly universal membership, the United Nations is a meeting-place of the states of the world and a symbol of world unity. The representatives of all states are forcibly reminded of the fact that their foreign policies and, increasingly, also their domestic affairs cannot be conducted exclusively in pursuit of selfish national aims. If the interests and feelings of other nations are affected, the issue comes under the discussion and scrutiny of the General Assembly. Every one of its members still pursues primarily an individual national interest, but the Assembly forces them to take other members into account as well. Many disputes and situations lose much of their potential danger when they receive publicity at an early stage, even though others thus become exacerbated.

When the General Assembly uneasily listens to acrimonious speeches and grapples with its overloaded agenda, perhaps it reflects a laborious but steady progress towards an international order which is gradually emerging from the countless permutations of the national interests voiced.

Non-global inter-governmental organizations

Much of the greatly increased post-war interaction has not been taking place at the global level but within a narrower scope, be it geographical regions or functional co-operation embracing only the states directly involved. To some extent these two bases have now fused and there is no marked difference between regional and functional organizations; indeed, the majority of regional organizations concentrate upon a specific function. If institutionalization can be regarded as a rough index of the intensity of interaction, more and more of the increased post-war international interaction takes place not at the global level; the non-global institutions all established after 1945, outnumber global ones. The distinguishing characteristic of these non-global, especially regional organizations, is that they tend to conduct their policies separately from the mainstream of global politics, although the latter occasionally intrude. The United Nations does not obstruct the trends towards regionalization; on the contrary, General Assembly sessions provide an additional opportunity for interaction and for voting together, whether to take a common stand on issues of common concern or to choose regional representatives.

A few relevant criteria for the evaluation of the role of a non-global inter-governmental organization in world politics can be found in the importance of its scope and domain and in the adequacy of its decision-making. The impact of the geographical scope is simple—an organization embracing nearly a whole continent is *prima facie* more important than one limited to a subregion: this is the relationship between the European Communities (E.E.C., 1958) and Benelux or the Organization of American States (O.A.S., 1948) and organizations in Central America, or the Organization for African Unity (O.A.U., 1963) and institutions in East or West Africa. The importance of the functional domain and of the weight of the organization within it is also clear. The E.E.C. is primarily engaged in world trade and is the largest world trader; the Organization of Petroleum Exporting Countries (OPEC, 1960) is concerned with oil production and distribution and includes the overwhelming majority of exporters; NATO and the Warsaw Pact are concerned with the major area of confrontation between East and West.

One has to consider also the capacity to act which is largely the function of the decision-making processes. In the past, much used to be made of the constitution of each organization, whether it assumed a 'supranational' character, i.e. was capable of making decisions binding on the members or dependent upon the consent of all members. The evolution of the E.E.C. since the so-called 'Luxembourg Compromise' has demonstrated the limitations of this distinction. Although constitutionally a majority vote is possible on some issues, a member can block the process whenever it deems that a vital national interest is at stake. Not only the constitutions but also another two variables are important: the size and the efficiency of the secretariat, and the cohesion of the membership and the degree to which they share basic attitudes on the issues within the ambit of the organization. For instance, OPEC's significance, great as it is owing to its domain, is diminished by the deep divisions among the moderate and the radical and the Arab and non-Arab members; the Warsaw Pact is dominated by the Soviet Union whereas NATO reflects a great degree of freedom of national behaviour which results in the absence of any significant standardization of arms and allows violent disputes between members to erupt.

Finally, one has to consider the dynamics of the organizations. Once functioning, they not only stabilize and often increase interaction within their scope but they also offer an established channel for additional interaction for which need may arise. This may take the form of the broadening of the geographical scope of the organization—for instance C.M.E.A. has included non-European members and Japan has been included in the international economic institutions originally limited to the Atlantic area. The extension can also be functional. For instance, being concerned with the Soviet military threat, NATO has also logically become the channel for the co-ordination of the members' general policies towards the Soviet Union. Perhaps most spectacular has been the functional extension of the E.E.C. to co-ordinate the foreign policies of the members beyond the areas of its competence. This has been limited only to informal periodical meetings of all the E.E.C. ambassadors in each capital and then extended to periodical meetings of the heads of the official machines of their foreign ministries. Although no decision-making is involved, exchange of information and views at the formative stage of policies constitutes an important step towards co-ordination, and may well eventually lead to the ultimate political unity sought by some members but opposed by others.

11 The problems of today and tomorrow

The new stakes of conflict

In order to facilitate comparisons, the post-war international system has already been briefly surveyed in terms of the 'stakes of conflict', used in a manner identical to that in the discussion of the preceding systems. This picture is not, of course, sufficient and has to be supplemented by a discussion of the new features distinguishing the contemporary system from its predecessors. What follows is a mere enumeration of the problems which appear to be of the greatest moment today and are likely to affect the future. Most of them have already been touched upon from different angles; their full assessment will, by necessity, have to await a historical perspective.

First of all, the post-war international system is characterized by a greatly increased *complexity* which is manifested in many ways. The actors have multiplied and have become heterogeneous in many essential respects: it is hard enough to conceptualize and understand the interaction among the more than 150 states now in existence, let alone all the new non-state actors, the exact roles of which are by no means clear. There is, moreover, a similar increase in the lines of conflict—the power political/ideological East/West conflict has developed partly separately and partly in interaction with the North/South conflict, while the issues of conflicts over resources sometimes constitute a separate domain and sometimes interact with either line or with both.

Second, it is important to note the greatly increased *intensity* of interaction. On the background of a rapidly developing technology, especially of transport, communications, and warfare, interaction across national boundaries has been growing with tremendous speed although this has been matched, and, in the case of the largest states, possibly even surpassed by a similar increase in domestic interaction. In absolute terms, however, international transactions have increased by a very large factor, according to any significant yardstick available: international trade, travel, diplomatic relations, etc.

Third, ours has been a period of very extensive and also very rapid *change*. There has been change in the nature of the major issues—e.g. the cold war has turned into a detente and the North/South conflict, which had started on the issue of anti-colonialism, still continuing about Southern Africa, has largely shifted to economic growth; there has been change in the salience of issue-areas—the gravity of international conflicts has moved from security to economics, resources, and ecopolitics—and the major danger spots which have gradually shifted from Europe to the Middle East and Africa; there has been change in the power and status of states—from a position of prostration China has become a Great Power following the Communist victory in 1949 and Japan and the Federal Republic of Germany have risen after their spectacular economic advance; following the rise in the price of oil in 1973, Saudi Arabia has acquired much larger liquid financial resources than those of any other state.

Closely connected is the fourth characteristic, of *dynamics*, the tendency for all the issues to grow, not only rapidly but also in size, or, as it is sometimes rather loosely put, 'exponentially'. The rise of the population of the earth from around 2,500,000 million in 1950 to around 4,500,000 million in the mid-seventies; the rise in the consumption of oil, the rise in the world expenditure on armaments to some U.S. $300,000 million by 1978 and of the calculated risks of casualties likely in a nuclear war to many 'mega-deaths', all testify to this tendency.

Fifth, *linkage between domestic and international affairs* has greatly grown in both directions. On the one hand, rapidly growing domestic needs and demands have become increasingly dependent upon international politics; on the other, international politics has become increasingly affected by domestic conflicts. The process can be conceptualized as diffusion, spill-over, or escalation and is particularly well-illustrated by the great growth of terrorism and hijacking from the sixties onwards.

Finally, the *instruments and agencies* of international order have not been able to keep pace with the changes. As this item is by no means self-explanatory, it requires some detail.

The two Superpowers have been performing the traditional

central role of keeping a degree of strategic equilibrium within the international system, but increasingly less effectively. This can be partly attributed to the growing difficulty of the task and partly to the increasing inadequacy of their resources for it and to the ineffectiveness of their leadership. When they had gained a degree of experience in dealing with each other, both Superpowers underwent severe setbacks in their domestic affairs and in the leadership of their respective blocs, although for quite different reasons. The phenomenon had several roots. There was, to start with, the economic strain. The Soviet economic system which had been highly effective although very costly in establishing heavy industry, was incapable of resolving the persisting difficulties with the collective arrangements in agriculture and with developing an effective light industry and a consumer goods distribution service. The Americans became increasingly dependent upon oil supplies, as their domestic sources ebbed while consumption continued to rise. While this resulted in large deficits in the balance of payments and in dependence on the external sources of supply, simultaneously the whole American industrial system, although highly efficient, came under an increasingly competitive foreign challenge while becoming simultaneously hampered by high labour costs and by ecological restrictions at home. Moreover, the ideologies in both countries suffered from traumatic events—dissidents ventured to question in public the adequacy of the protection of human rights in the Soviet Union while the United States went through, and largely overcame, great domestic turmoil over Vietnam and then over Watergate.

It is understandable that the capacity for international leadership of both Superpowers was impaired by the weakening of their domestic bases, in a world in which the national paths towards Communism—notably in Yugoslavia, China, and lately, Western Europe—had defied Soviet direction, while the Americans likewise lost the sense of manifest destiny, a clear-cut role in the world, and their leadership of the Western bloc had been weakened mainly owing to their relative loss of economic power, the strategic doctrine of 'graduated deterrence' which made their nuclear protection less certain, their severe setback in Vietnam, and their inability to stand up to Communist advances in Africa.

No wonder both blocs showed signs of loosening; China became seemingly permanently estranged from Russia.

Simultaneously international arrangements were negotiated and international institutions established to cope with a variety of the new tasks, often with great ingenuity but, on the whole, with success limited mainly to technical matters. Certainly the United Nations has not fulfilled the early expectations of its enthusiasts and has proved incapable either of resolving acute international conflicts or of co-ordinating a fully-fledged international co-operation.

There is no simple way of bringing all these characteristics of the contemporary international system into a comprehensive framework of analysis. This is best demonstrated by the fact that a different periodization is required by each angle from which one may undertake the analysis. From the systemic point of view, the stability of the security and of the economic systems seems to indicate opposed trends: after a period of acute cold war, relative stability in the former and, after a period of sustained economic growth, a definite slowing down with the dangers of stagnation and even collapse in the late seventies. The picture looks quite different from other points of view. Thus, in the Atlantic bloc, both in the areas of security and of economics, periodization would be most convincingly based upon the vigorous exercise of American leadership in the early post-war period and its weakening in the sixties and seventies. From national points of view, however, the crucial events for each nation are different: Vietnam and Watergate for the Americans, Suez for the British, change of leadership—Stalin, Khrushchev, Mao, Tito—in Communist states; independence and the death or removal of the first leader or generation of leaders, in new states.

Capacity for problem-solving

Another even more fundamental effect of the confusion in the contemporary international system is the mixture of elements conducive both to its stability and its instability. This is best demonstrated by a few concrete examples. The so-called 'cold war' has undoubtedly been the central issue of post-war international politics, leading both to pessimistic forecasts of an inevitable clash between the two titans which would engulf mankind in a real catastrophe, and to optimistic ideas about the possibility of accommodation. As decades pass, neither estimate has proved right. On the one hand, the two Superpowers came to several 'eyeball-to-eyeball' confrontations, especially during the Cuban Missile Crisis in 1962, but gradually they engaged in a slow but distinct detente. On the other, the basic hostility and difficulty of accommodation remained strongly in evidence.

If one distinguishes between the power political and the ideological roots of this central conflict, it seems inevitable that the two dominant Powers would engage in military and political competition but the tendency towards rigid bipolarity in the immediate post-war decade was later replaced by a tendency towards polycentrism. Likewise the clash between the commanding collectivist ideology of the Soviet Union and the individualist one of the United States inevitably exacerbates the antagonism, but the edges of both ideologies have now become greatly blurred. The fundamental differences between them are narrowing somewhat; perhaps it is significant that both are the offspring of the ideas of the Enlightenment about social progress based upon rationalism. The Americans, despite their fears of 'creeping socialism' have introduced a range of collectivist arrangements for social welfare while, from the seventies, the Soviet rulers have come under increasing domestic pressures for greater individual freedom and for protection of human rights. Finally, centrally important common interests have emerged: both the Russians and the Americans have firmly recognized that they should avoid a nuclear war; although somewhat reluctantly, as developed industrialized countries they have occasionally come close to a common stand on North/South issues; they have also engaged in increased trade-exchanges—to provide a much-needed access to the Western technology to the Russians and equally much-needed additional markets to the West.

The nature of Soviet/American relations is most clearly revealed in the field of armaments. Once the Russians had achieved a 'second-strike capability', meaning a nuclear force capable of surviving an American nuclear attack and striking back, a basic stability had been reached, despite the uncertainties engendered by technological innovation. The relationship is, however, infinitely more complex than the balance of power in the nineteenth century. This is manifested by the great variety of levels at which the issue of armaments is dealt with: most important are the bilateral Strategic Arms Limitations Talks (SALT) but simultaneously there are going on NATO/Warsaw Pact Mutual Balanced Force Reduction (M.B.F.R.) talks and global United Nations Disarmament talks, and, occasionally, international conferences are held. There has been some ostensible technical progress towards a degree of containment of armaments—e.g. the prickly question of inspection, which involves accepting a crucial breach in the prerogatives of sovereignty, has been largely resolved by the increasingly effective surveillance from satellites and, through a series of treaties, the testing of nuclear weapons has been circumscribed. The negotiations at the various levels have not, however, been uncoordinated and there is a strong element of unreality in all of them: often quite unrealistic aspirations continue to be professed; sales and grants of ever more sophisticated weapons to a growing number of states are becoming an increasingly disruptive element in regional arms balances; China and quite a few other potential and actual possessors of nuclear weapons refuse to become bound by the nuclear agreements; potentially equally lethal biological and chemical weapons, though proscribed, are probably being developed; perhaps most importantly, during the seventies the pace and scope of technological change made questionable the use of any agreements whatsoever.

Intractable conflicts of the traditional type, over territory and political independence, continue to abound. The most prominent among these has been the Arab/Israeli conflict which led to four major Middle Eastern wars over a long period in 1947, 1956, 1967, and 1973. The fundamental nature of this conflict has remained identical but the identity of the actors has been constantly changing, fluctuating between a largely regional context and a global one. The protagonists were at first Israel and the Arab 'confrontation states', in close proximity; then the P.L.O. became an important agent but it was considerably weakened in the late seventies owing to inner splits; first the British and the French, then the Russians and finally the Americans became involved; the United Nations played an intermittent part.

An incredible variety of diplomatic procedures was employed.

Many of them were under the auspices of the United Nations: armistice commissions, 'proximity talks' between the Arabs and the Israelis—as the former refused to deal with the latter directly—U.N. resolutions, missions by U.N. Special Representatives, the round-table Geneva Conference. There were also high-level bilateral meetings, first in secret, and then, since President Sadat's visit to Israel in 1977, official and public; there were, finally, repeated American initiatives, notably a long period of 'shuttle diplomacy' under Dr. Kissinger, and in 1978, a trilateral summit meeting between the leaders of Israel and Egypt and the President of the U.S., at the latter's invitation. The basic conflict between Israel and the Arabs boils down to the traditional issues of security and territory; despite all the regional and international efforts it seemed impossible to find terms for a concrete arrangement to produce a mutually acceptable bargain between Israel's demands for security and Arab demands for the return of territories occupied by Israel in 1967. The richness of diplomatic inventiveness did not prevent recurrent outbreaks of violence or the possibility of its escalation to a global level, though led to the Egypt-Israel Peace Treaty of March 1979.

Equally futile were the international attempts to deal with the problems of terrorism, especially the hijacking of planes, which erupted in the sixties and seventies. Given the internationalization of the phenomenon and the support of a few states willing to offer arms, training facilities and a sanctuary, and also the widespread acceptance of the legitimacy of some 'liberation organizations' engaged in the terrorist activities, it has proved impossible to reach any effective international agreements. The repeated expressions of the need for them have remained in the realm of aspirations.

To turn now to the field of international economics, the economists engaged in determining the technical forms have been even more inventive than the diplomats and, temporarily, much more successful. The international economic system of the market economics—established at Bretton Woods in 1944—worked effectively for some quarter of a century, largely aided by the large initial United States aid and by its being based on the generally acceptable principle of increasingly freer trade. It was limited to the non-Communist countries but embraced most of international trade and finance and it worked apparently autonomously, while the political system was centring on the conflicts of the cold war.

The post-war rehabilitation was rapid, economic growth took place in all industrialized countries, in some of them, especially Japan and the Federal Republic of Germany, at a prodigious rate, while international trade was growing at double the rate of the economic growth. The growth could not, however, be kept up indefinitely and the Bretton Woods system disintegrated in the seventies because it could not cope with new forces—the economic surge of the E.E.C. and Japan, the consequences of the oil crisis, the challenge to the domination of international trade by the Western industrialized countries by Japan and then also other newly industrialized states, the inability of the former to control industrial costs, inflation and unemployment, and, perhaps most importantly, the relative weakening of American economic supremacy resulting in the drastic devaluation of the dollar and the loss of American leadership.

As in the field of security, the variety of agencies and instruments devised to cope with economics was enormous. The most important of these were the Organization for Economic Co-operation and Development (O.E.C.D.), a loose umbrella organization of the whole Western world, and the E.E.C., the more tightly binding regional organization of Western Europe. National sovereignty did not obstruct a degree of international management in economics as starkly as in the field of security and, indeed, the international economic system weathered several severe crises. Notably, through establishing special oil credit facilities, the International Monetary Fund (I.M.F.) maintained a degree of stability in the international monetary system after the global balances of payments had been drastically and fundamentally disturbed by the quadrupling of the price of oil in 1973. In the late seventies, it became an important international agent in curbing inflation by making the large credit facilities required from it by many members conditional upon anti-inflationary governmental policies. Perhaps even more spectacular was the relatively limited turn away from the principle of a free international trade by states threatened by large trade deficits—the recession in international trade did not, therefore, result in a return to the disastrous protectionism and trade wars of the thirties. Characteristically, in the late seventies, the loose management of international economics became somewhat institutionalized by the periodic summit meetings of the leaders of the major industrialized Powers, an institution basically resembling the operation of the Concert of Europe immediately after the Napoleonic Wars.

Much more complex and unmanageable was the North/South confrontation due to the demands of the developing countries for a 'New International Economic Order' in which they would secure better conditions for development, especially through better terms of trade and substantial aid. The industrialized countries reluctantly accepted the principle. They gave aid, though less than demanded, and made limited trade arrangements by allowing developing states a somewhat privileged position under the terms of the General Agreement on Trade and Tariffs (G.A.T.T.) and also under successive conventions concluded by the E.E.C. In the seventies the situation became further complicated by the world recession resulting in drastic falls in commodity prices and by the predicament of the poorest nations faced with swollen oil bills; the latter problem was largely met by grants from the members of OPEC. The basic cohesion of the Group of 77, organizing the Less Developed States now risen to over a hundred, did not, however, reach the previous cohesion of the Third World over anticolonialism. This was understandable in the light of the increasing economic disparities between the incomes of the oil-exporters who have remained members, although they had become the richest nations on earth as the result of their oil-earnings, and the consistent poverty of others. Moreover, it was becoming increasingly clear that effective relief of poverty could not be achieved by international action alone because it requires a rational restructuring of the economies and hence also the societies of the Third World. Effective action in this direction was not within the power of the industrialized countries and they were politically inhibited even in making demands for it as a condition for further concessions. Finally, by the seventies, both the Western and the Communist models of economic development had become tarnished by the adverse experiences of both systems.

The rapid growth of population and of world economies since the War raised the spectre of several possible dangers to the future of mankind which were widely publicized by the influential volume *Limits to Economic Growth*, produced by the Club of Rome, and by numerous subsequent analyses. Although the recession of the seventies slowed down the hitherto incessantly growing demands for food and raw materials, especially oil, the question remained insoluble how the demands of the Third World states, following the same path of industrialization as the Europeans, could possibly be met. This was by no means an impossible contingency, especially when, after Mao's death, the rulers of China decided to turn to the West for help with modernization and industrialization. It is important, however, to stress also the other side of the picture. Internationally concerted action was only occasionally attempted, generally by the United Nations, and often did not go beyond exchanges of views and sometimes statements of principles. Nevertheless, the ecological disasters prophesied did not take place, mainly as the result of the operation of market forces, some relatively uncoordinated national activities and the diffusion of ideas and of technology. Thus despite low standards of nutrition and occasional famines, a near-balance between population and food was achieved through a slowing down of population increases due to urban pressures, as well as through a combination of deliberate governmental policies and of the development of high-yield hybrid grains and greater use of artificial fertilizers. The rapidly growing energy demands were satisfied by oil, which largely replaced coal; when oil shortage was looming in the seventies, many more sources of oil supply were found and exploited, most spectacularly from the sea-bed; even when world oil supplies were temporarily cut during the Yom Kippur war in 1973, distribution was efficiently continued by the major oil companies; awareness of the dangers of pollution spread so widely during the seventies that pressure of public opinion halted and possibly reversed its increase in the industrialized countries. Thus, despite our inability to secure concerted international action and our lateness in responding to problems, mankind has so far weathered the ecological and resources crises and near-crises much better than could reasonably have been expected.

Prospects

The few examples of current international problems hitherto discussed are scarcely adequate for giving a full idea of the complexity of the contemporary international system. They do, nevertheless, allow us to make an informed guess about the possible direction in the evolution of this system towards the end of the twentieth century.

This book started with a working hypothesis that mankind is loosely organized into an international society of sovereign states which rely mainly, although not exclusively, on power in their mutual relations. These states are represented by individuals holding certain official positions who determine state policies under the complex, often conflicting influences and pressures from their domestic and international environments. Inevitably, international society is subject to repeated crises and to the recurrent danger of war; it cannot effectively cope with a growing number of political, economic and ecological problems, although lately co-operation among states in all these fields has been growing.

We are undoubtedly faced with a major crisis of the territorial sovereign state in its traditional form. No state is any longer self-sufficient or safe within its boundaries, not even the Superpowers, let alone the new mini-states; all are facing a diminution of their sovereignty. Nevertheless, it is hard to see how the present division of mankind into states could readily lose its importance in the foreseeable future. This supposition readily leads to one possible future—an international system continuing much as it is now, although with states probably somewhat readier to co-ordinate their activities at the cost of further inroads into their sovereignty, and new non-state actors and transnational activities further supplementing their activities. Envisaging such a future may, however, be no more than a simplistic, and naïve, projection into the future of the trends of the present and of the immediate past. Legitimate doubts about the validity of this forecast can be raised on the basis both of the seriousness of the individual problems with which the system will have to cope and the cumulative effect of their number.

The only rational model for the future would be one of some form of world government. Without it no satisfactory solution to the core problems of our times can be envisaged—whether ensuring the prevention of a major war or some form of world-wide economic growth with a degree of re-distribution and without disastrous ecological by-effects—because all of these require political decisions not limited to individual nations but within the

global or some broad regional context. Although this is acknow-
ledged not only by theoreticians but also quite frequently and
openly by statesmen, advance from our plural system to a unitary
one seems not only to be politically impossible but, on reflection,
also undesirable. Even within individual states unification for
basic political purposes has been achieved at the cost of overriding
the interests and aspirations of some of the various subgroups and
minorities. Pressures for supranational solution of broader than
national problems are nowadays matched by pressure for subnational solution of problems peculiar to national subgroups. A
wholesale or even only a substantial transfer of powers to a supranational authority could further aggravate the existing subnational conflicts and would add to them a new and even more
important layer of national ones.

There is, however, also a third future international order possible which would combine some features of the two already discussed and could therefore be both more feasible and more effective
than either. For lack of a better term we could call it one of 'mixed
management'. On the one hand, it would be firmly based upon the
present pluralist system of mixed actors, with states being most
prominent among them; on the other, it would introduce an element of rational planning for international order, both at the
global and at regional levels. It is possible to interpret the present
situation as being the initial stage of such a system. States still
occupy a central position as the sovereign entities with the ultimate
power of political decision, but are rapidly adjusting their authority in two directions: delegating it both to some broader
bodies—global and regional—to deal with problems with which
the state on its own is helpless, and downwards, where minorities
feel dissatisfied and press for devolution. In order to avoid arid
debates over sovereignty and its clashes, it may be useful to think
about such a system in terms of functional needs and of what may
be termed delegation sideways, not through accepting supra- or
transnational authority but through completely depoliticizing
some politically less sensitive activities and having them run by
international or transnational organizations; the Universal Postal
Union provides a good example.

There is general agreement about a desirable broad direction—that international order should ensure freedom from a major

war, economic growth without disastrous ecological effects, and some minimum human rights. There is, however, basic disagreement about the appropriate means for securing these major objectives, as expressed in the varying lines of contemporary conflicts. It would be unrealistic, therefore, to expect that any rationally designed major international policies would command general acceptance. In the light of the post-war experience it seems, nevertheless, quite realistic to expect that actual or anticipated severe crises in specific fields and on specific issues may lead to global or regional action and ultimately institutionalization. If the experience of the E.E.C. can serve as a guide, in the longer run it seems likely that the states will delegate some of their authority upwards, although this is likely to take place in an erratic fashion and not according to a blueprint, and also be obstructed by reversions to an assertion of national sovereignty. It is relatively easy to classify the factors which will determine the future shape of the international system. They fall into the categories of functional needs, political will, and a residual group of random though often important elements, but it seems impossible to evaluate with any degree of certainty how these elements will shape and interact.

Thus prediction about the likely shape of the international system at the end of the twentieth century is bound to be not only impressionistic but vague: the system will be pluralistic and untidy and the states will continue to play an important though probably diminishing role, the exact extent of which cannot even be guessed.

Reading List

Allison, G. T., *Essence of Decision*, Boston, Massachusetts, 1971. A systematic analysis of decision-making in the Cuban Missile Crisis.

Aron, R., *Peace and War*, Weidenfeld & Nicolson, 1966. A comprehensive philosophical and sociological analysis.

Bergsten, F. & Krause, L., eds., *World Politics and International Economics*, 1976. A lucid introduction to the subject.

Bull, H., *The Anarchical Society*, Macmillan, 1977. An analysis of the main issues of world order.

Burton, J. W., *World Society*, Cambridge, 1972. An introduction to conceptualization and analysis.

Calvacoressi, P., *World Politics since 1945*, 3rd edn., Longman, 1977. A brief introduction to the post-war political history.

Carr, E. H., *The Twenty Years' Crisis, 1919–1939*, 2nd edn., Macmillan, 1946. Now a classical analysis of the inter-war period.

Claude, I. L., Jr., *Swords into Plowshares*, 3rd edn., University of London Press, 1964. A searching analysis of international organization.

Clausewitz, K. V., *On War*, Princeton University Press, 1976. A classic on the subject.

Deutsch, K. W., *The Analysis of International Relations*, 2nd edn., Prentice-Hall, 1978. An introduction employing concepts of modern political science.

Frankel, J., *The Making of Foreign Policy*, Oxford, 1962. An analysis of decision-making, stressing values.

International Politics: Conflict and Harmony, Penguin, 1969. An analysis focusing on the two modes of state interaction.

National Interest, 1970. An analysis of the central concern governing state behaviour.

Contemporary International Theory and the Behaviour of States, Oxford, 1973. A brief and simple introduction.

Henkin, L., *How Nations Behave: Law and Foreign Policy*, Pall Mall, 1968. A lucid analysis of the interaction of the two.

Herz, J., *International Politics in the Nuclear Age*, Columbia University

Press, 1959. An analysis centring on the crisis of the territorial state.

Holsti, K. J., *International Politics*, 3rd edn., 1978. A fairly full and well balanced general text-book.

Joll, J., *Europe since 1870*, 2nd edn., Weidenfeld & Nicolson and Penguin, 1976. A well-balanced, brief survey of political history.

Kaplan, M. A., *System and Process in International Relations*, New York, 1957. The first, now classical, application of system analysis.

Kenwood, A. G. & Lougheed, A. L., *Growth of the International Economy 1820–1960*, Allen & Unwin, 1971. An introduction to economic history.

Machiavelli, *The Prince*. The classical work on power politics (any edition).

Morgenthau, H., *Politics Among Nations*, 5th edn., New York, 1975. A leading American text-book based on the power-political approach.

Reynolds, C., *Theory and Explanation in International Politics*, Martin Robertson, London, 1973. An introduction to the philosophical issues of explanation.

Schelling, T. C., *The Strategy of Conflict*, Oxford, 1963. An application of the bargaining theory and analysis of the policy of deterrence.

Snyder, R. C. and others, *Foreign Policy Decision Making*, New York, 1962. The first, now classical, outline of the decision-making approach.

Thucydides, *History of the Peloponnesian War*. A classical analytical history (any edition).

Waltz, K. J., *Man, The State and War*, Columbia University Press, 1959. A systematic analysis of classical political theory on the causes of war.

Periodicals

BRITISH

British Journal of International Studies (quarterly)
International Affairs (quarterly)
Millennium (quarterly)
World Today (monthly)

AMERICAN

American Political Science Review (quarterly)
Foreign Affairs (quarterly)
Foreign Policy (quarterly)
International Organization (four-monthly)
Journal of Conflict Resolution (quarterly)
World Politics (quarterly)

Index